WILD KINGDOM

STEPHEN MOSS

WILD KINGDOM

Bringing Back Britain's Wildlife

SQUARE PEG

LONDON

1 3 5 7 9 10 8 6 4 2

Square Peg, an imprint of Vintage,
20 Vauxhall Bridge Road,
London SW1V 2SA

Square Peg is part of the Penguin Random House group of companies
whose addresses can be found at global.penguinrandomhouse.com

First published by Square Peg in 2016

www.vintage-books.co.uk

A CIP catalogue record for this book
is available from the British Library

ISBN 9780224095655

Typeset in India by Thomson Digital Pvt Ltd, Noida, Delhi
Printed and bound in Great Britain by Clays Ltd, St Ives plc

Penguin Random House is committed to a sustainable future for our
business, our readers and our planet. This book is made from Forest
Stewardship Council® certified paper.

For Derek Moore, 1943–2014
Conservationist, birder, mentor and friend

Contents

INTRODUCTION

How much is a view worth? How do you cost account a landscape? Can a computer be programmed to evaluate bird song and the brief choreography of a young beech plantation against a May sky, a kestrel hovering in winter air? Is there a method of reckoning up the percentage in a person's inner replenishment from wild country?

Kenneth Allsop, *In the Country* (1972)

A DEEP, BOOMING sound, like a distant foghorn, resonates deep in the reed bed. Behind me a mechanical buzzing stops and starts: an angler reeling out his line, or an insect, perhaps? In the skies above, a loud honking, as two enormous birds drift overhead. Down below, an elegant, long-necked, Persil-white creature stands stock-still, before plunging a dagger-like bill into the water to spear a fish, its death throes glistening in the bright June sunshine.

Bittern, Savi's warbler, a pair of cranes and a great white egret: four species of bird that have, during the past decade, made their home in the Avalon Marshes in Somerset. Four species that, until recently, were either very rare or completely absent from Britain. Now they live out their lives in a wetland created from an old industrial site; former peat diggings within sight of Glastonbury Tor.

1

Ten years ago, I moved with my young family down to Somerset from London. When we exchanged the metropolitan rat race for a more tranquil and fulfilling life in the English countryside, I knew that I was also swapping swifts for swallows, parakeets for lapwings, and insolent urban foxes for shy rural ones. What I didn't realise was that, before a decade was out, I would witness a complete transformation of this landscape and its wildlife.

When we moved into our new home, on the hottest day of the hottest month on record, none of these new arrivals was here. All have since colonised this corner of the West Country, adopting this magical landscape as their own.

They are not alone: each spring and summer, the air resounds with the calling of cuckoos, the buzzing of dragonflies and the hidden presence of hawkmoths. In autumn and winter, crowds gather to witness the massive murmurations of starlings performing their aerobatic displays as dusk falls.

Now, the wildlife is spreading out into the surrounding parishes. As I write, a buzzard is perched on our garden goalpost, where my children practise their football skills. On a December bike ride around the fields behind our house I see barn owls and bullfinches, bouncing roe deer and lithe, fast-moving stoats, and the occasional peregrine, cruising over the fields in search of its prey. In June the verges of the lanes are awash with cow parsley and the pinkish-purple flowers of great willowherb; while whitethroats shoot up from the hedgerows to deliver their scratchy song, and skylarks hang even higher in the azure skies. If there is a better place to live in Britain – an even more wildlife-rich landscape, with so many exciting new inhabitants – then I'd love to know about it. In the meantime, for me, this is pretty close to paradise.

❀

AND YET . . . IN the wider world, beyond my immediate horizons, I know that nature is not faring so well. The newspaper headlines, the reports and surveys, and the anecdotal evidence of so many people I meet and talk to, tell a very different tale. In much of Britain's countryside, our wildlife is in big trouble. Species that have lived here for thousands of years are disappearing, under threat from pollution and persecution, competition with alien invaders, changing farming and forestry practices, and climate change.

During my own lifetime – barely fifty years since I first became aware of the wild creatures with which we share this small island – I have seen changes that could never have been foreseen. Who would have thought that house sparrows and hedgehogs, both so common and widespread that we simply took them for granted, would have suffered such catastrophic population declines? Who would have believed that generations of children would now be growing up without ever hearing the call of the cuckoo, a sound that for our rural ancestors marked the coming of spring? And who would ever have imagined that hares and skylarks, water voles and bumblebees, turtle doves and partridges, would all be in danger of disappearing from our rural landscape? It is clear that if we don't do something to stem these declines – and soon – we may lose some of our most charismatic creatures for ever.

What has happened to Britain's countryside and its wildlife? How have we managed to create new landscapes, and attract such exciting new arrivals, at a time when so many of our wild creatures are under threat? Why and how did much of the British countryside turn into a wildlife-free zone? And now, at the eleventh hour, what can we do to turn the tide of decline and disappearance, bring these species back from the brink, and restore the special places where they live?

❀

THIS BOOK ASKS a simple question, with a rather more complex answer: Can Britain make room for wildlife?

I believe we can. And the fightback has already begun. All over the country, people are working hard to save the plants and animals they love. Thanks to the efforts of an army of volunteers, with expert help from professional conservationists, otters have returned to our rivers, red kites are flying over our woodlands, and the peregrine –

the fastest living creature on the planet – has taken up residence in our urban jungles, including the centre of London itself. In small pockets of the British countryside things are at last beginning to change too. What were once nature-free zones are being 'rewilded'; giving our wild creatures the space they need, as nature begins its long, slow battle against the forces that would destroy it.

As we begin this fightback, we also need to understand that the natural world can no longer be regarded as a bolt-on luxury. Not only does it contribute to the economy, it is also absolutely essential for our well-being, as individuals, in communities and for the nation as a whole. Getting close to nature on a regular basis makes us more happy and fulfilled in our lives, healthier and helps us live longer. Helping wild creatures return really is a win-win solution: one that benefits not just the wildlife, but the places and people too.

❁

THIS BOOK IS the product of many journeys I have made through Britain during the past few decades, to take stock of our wildlife and the state of our countryside. I've travelled from the Somerset Levels to Shetland, the River Tyne to a Dorset chalk stream, and the centre of London to the wilds of the Scottish Highlands. I've visited the astonishing range of habitats we have on these islands, from farmland to woodland, mountain to moorland, and rivers to the sea, and enjoyed unforgettable encounters with the wild creatures that live there. I've also visited the unexpected havens for wildlife in our towns and cities, along with the 'accidental countryside': roadside verges and railway cuttings, golf courses and gravel pits, military sites and churchyards – often unappreciated places, where many of our plants and animals have found a safe refuge. Along the way I've come across devastation and rebirth, witnessed comebacks and declines, and met countless passionate people who are doing their very best to help Britain's wildlife.

This is also a journey through time. My story begins more than 5,000 years ago, when the first settlers started to transform our largely wooded landscape into something more open and more varied than before. I outline the great changes brought about as human beings began to dominate the landscape, from the draining of the Fens, through the growth of our cities during the Industrial Revolution, to the post-war era, when change rapidly accelerated as nature and wildlife took a back seat to economic growth. And in the final chapter, I look to the future: a future in which wildlife finally has the chance to thrive.

Finally, this is a very personal journey. I have been passionate about the natural world for as long as I can remember. In the half-century since then, my love of nature, and my understanding and appreciation of it, has grown and grown. This happened slowly at first, but as time has gone on, I have finally come to appreciate just how much I depend on the wild creatures, the landscapes and the special places around me. So this book is imbued with my own, very personal, response to what has happened to Britain's wildlife: with my own passions and prejudices, fears and hopes, and wishes and ambitions for the land I love, and the wonderful plants and animals that live here.

STEPHEN MOSS

Mark, Somerset, September 2015

1

Down on the Farm

Farmland and Grassland

To many of us, heaven might be the meadows of
Edwardian England, the big blue sky, the haycocks
a-drying, the clean river running by; while we laze in the
sun, read poetry and listen to the bees and skylarks.

Peter Marren, *British Wildlife* (1995)

ONE MORNING, ROUGHLY 5,000 years ago, a young
man went to work on what we now call the Marlborough
Downs, in the county of Wiltshire. As the sun rose over
the distant hillside to the east, he took out a long, narrow
blade carefully shaped from a piece of flint, and knelt
down by a stone.

Leaning forward, he placed the flint into a groove
already cut in the stone's surface, and began to sharpen
it. Finally, satisfied that the tool was ready for the job in
hand, he set about the day's task: cutting down trees to
create an open clearing, where he and his companions
could plant seeds to grow crops.

This long-forgotten man was one of the earliest
farmers, the first in an unbroken line of individuals and

communities who have worked our land to provide food for themselves, their families, and – in later eras – for the rest of us.

Standing by this same stone and looking across this vast, open, windswept landscape, I find it almost impossible to imagine what this place would have looked like before those first people settled here. Today, these rolling hills and downlands are the quintessential farmed landscape of lowland England: what we know and cherish as a picture-postcard image of 'the countryside'.

We take comfort from the apparently unchanging nature of this scene; and yet if we dig a little deeper into its history, we soon discover that, like most of Britain, there is nothing remotely natural about it at all. Everything I can see, all around me, has been shaped – and indeed is still being shaped – by human hand.

So although we think of Britain's farmed countryside as somehow traditional, consistent and unchanging, it is anything but. It is crucial that we bear this in mind when we contemplate the state of Britain's wild creatures and the places where they live, and try to decide what we can do to bring them back from the brink.

❁

To REALLY APPRECIATE the way that successive generations of farmers have transformed the landscape I only need to travel a few miles north of the Marlborough

Downs, and take the M4 motorway towards London. On both sides of the road, for mile after mile, the predominant colour is green: a patchwork quilt of various shades, occasionally broken by a square of wheat or barley, or the electric yellow of oilseed rape; but mainly the green of highly fertilised grass grown for grazing or silage.

In the words of cultural historian Michel Pastoureau, green is 'a ubiquitous and soothing presence as the symbol of environmental causes and the mission to save the planet'. But this vivid emerald hue, stretching as far as my eyes can see, has nothing natural about it at all. This dazzling green is the colour of intensive farming. By associating it with something positive and 'natural', as many continue to do, we become blind to its real meaning.

Try this simple experiment: look across an intensively farmed landscape, almost anywhere in lowland Britain, and imagine that every green field you can see is a vivid, luminous red – the colour we associate with danger. Now imagine seeing field after field of magenta, scarlet and crimson, stretching off into the distance like a scene from some manic film-maker's futuristic apocalypse. You might not be so inclined to regard our farmed countryside in quite the same way.

The reason this is so important is because it covers more than twice as much land as all our other wildlife habitats combined. Indeed, roughly three quarters of the whole of Britain's land area is defined as 'farmland'. From the arable fields of the lowlands to the hill farms of the uplands, this vast area – about 70,000 square miles in all – is used to grow crops, raise livestock, produce timber or, increasingly, for wind and solar power. Without question this is by far the most important habitat in the country – not just for wildlife, but for Britain's 64 million people too. This is also what we call the countryside.

The *Oxford English Dictionary* defines the word 'countryside' as 'the land and scenery of a rural area'; while its *Cambridge* equivalent expresses the concept in rather more passive terms: 'Land not in towns, cities or industrial areas, that is either used for farming or left in its natural condition.'

But neither of these definitions gets anywhere near capturing the profound resonance of the word 'countryside' to the British ear. This resonance is shaped by memories of our early childhood, poring over picture books showing kindly Farmer Jim on his bright red tractor, surrounded by happy-looking hens, pigs and cows. It is fuelled by the cultural connections of the word, from the poetry of Keats to the music of Vaughan Williams. And it is reinforced each day, as we are bombarded with bucolic images on advertising hoardings, which exploit our deep love of the countryside to sell us everything from milk to mortgages.

These images and cultural associations take us far beyond any prosaic meaning of the word 'countryside'. Together they conjure up a rose-tinted view of rural Britain held dear by millions; one that is shamelessly exploited by self-appointed, minority-interest pressure groups whose claim to be the guardians of the countryside would be amusing, were its consequences not so serious.

Although this simple word evokes a sense of pride, warmth and affection in the hearts of millions of Britons, we need to think again. The truth is that the vast majority of our lowland countryside is a factory, producing food to sell to the supermarkets and manufacturers, food that will eventually go into our shopping baskets and end up on our dinner tables.

Farmers will tell you that their primary job is to produce food, and they are right. What they may not tell you is that under the current system, in which the supermarkets and wholesalers continually force down the prices they pay farmers for their produce, in order to provide cheaper food for us (and better profits for their shareholders), the farmers themselves have little or no choice but to maximise their yields by using every means possible.

In practice this has meant removing hedgerows to create larger and larger fields, ploughing up field margins so they can plant up to the very edge of the land, and continually spraying with poisonous herbicides and insecticides to wipe out any wild flowers or insects that might compete with their precious crops.

This approach certainly works: it enables Britain's farmers to maximise their resources and produce food at the price that retailers and consumers demand. But it has two major problems. First, that however hard they work, and however much they increase their production, most of Britain's farmers see little or no profit for their efforts. No wonder that so many of them are struggling to survive, or simply going out of business.

The other problem is that modern intensive farming leaves little or no room for the plants and animals that have shared this rural space with us for thousands of years: the birds and mammals, bees and butterflies, grasses and wild flowers of the British countryside.

❀

TAKE A WALK along a public footpath across open, intensively farmed arable land almost anywhere in East Anglia during the spring or summer, and you'll soon be struck by an odd sense of something wrong. It may take you a while to put your finger on what this is, but after a few minutes it will dawn on you that one important thing is missing: birdsong.

In the bright skies, where distant skylarks should hang in the air, pouring out their song like a leaky tap: silence. In the hedgerows – if you can find one – where whitethroats should be launching themselves skywards and singing their scratchy little tune: silence. And along the edges, where unseen partridges should be revealing their presence by their harsh, grating call, again, all is silent.

Apart from the gently waving heads of corn in the summer's breeze, there is an eerie stillness. Nothing moves. The flutter of butterflies, their colours catching the eye as they reflect the sunshine; the buzz of bumblebees, as they flit from flower to flower; even the flowers themselves – the crimson petals of the poppy, the intense blue spikes of the cornflower, the delicate pinkish-purple of the corncockle – are all absent. In the corncockle's case, this arable weed which was once widespread is now virtually extinct in the wild in Britain.

It's not the only familiar farmland species that has disappeared from vast swathes of the countryside. At first glance, a corn bunting looks rather like a sparrow that has let itself go to seed: a plump, brown, streaky bird with an unkempt plumage and a tuneless, jangling song. The corn bunting is so closely associated with the farmed landscape that, like the cornflower and the corncockle, our ancestors named it after our most important arable crops.

But in many parts of Britain, the corn bunting's song is now but a distant memory: nine out of ten corn buntings have vanished since 1970, and their breeding range has contracted by more than half during the same period. The same story can be told about the turtle dove, the grey partridge, the yellowhammer – even the once-ubiquitous skylark. During my own lifetime, roughly 2 million pairs of skylarks have simply disappeared; and the same is true of many other farmland birds, such as the tree sparrow, yellow wagtail and grey partridge, whose numbers have fallen by four fifths in the past forty years.

Worryingly, these declines appear to be accelerating, despite efforts to make farming more wildlife-friendly. So the turtle dove, a bird once so familiar that it appears with the partridge in the celebrated song 'The Twelve Days of Christmas', is now predicted to disappear as a British bird by the year 2021. If the corn bunting's decline continues, it won't be far behind.

But statistics only tell part of the story. It is the reality on the ground that really brings home the scale of these declines. Where once Britain's fields echoed to the jangling of the 'fat bird of the barley', or the distinctive purring of the turtle dove, they are now often silent.

These birds are just the most visible tip of a very large iceberg. For all our farmland wildlife, the changes that have taken place over the past seventy years or so have been nothing short of catastrophic. As the countryside has become industrialised, simplified and homogenised, so wildlife has lost the variety of landscapes it needs to survive: the hidden corners where creatures can hide from predators, the hedgerows where they can raise a family, the ponds where they drink, the stubble fields where they feed in winter, have all vanished. In their place, we have what is an agricultural desert: vast monocultures of single crops such as wheat or barley stretching for hectare after hectare, with barely a hedgerow or tree left standing to break the monotony.

It's easy to look at today's countryside and assume that things can't be quite as bad as conservationists make out. But we only need to find out what we have lost since the end of the Second World War to realise just how much has vanished. During the past seventy years – the span of a single human lifetime – we have lost 99 per cent of our hay meadows, 96 per cent of our chalk and limestone grasslands, half a million farm ponds, and 300,000 miles of our hedgerows – enough to stretch from the earth to way beyond the moon.

For children growing up today, indeed for most of us who cannot remember back more than a few decades, the countryside may appear as if it has been the same for centuries. But those who can still recall the years between the wars know that our rural landscape was very different then: richer, more varied, and above all filled with a far greater variety of plants and insects, mammals and birds. This is not mere rose-tinted nostalgia – but a glimpse of the reality of what modern industrial farming has done to our countryside.

How have we managed to preside over such a cataclysmic decline in our farmland wildlife, a decline that may not be reversible? How have successive governments, conservationists, farmers and the people of Britain – many of whom care deeply about the natural world and would staunchly defend the importance of the British countryside – allowed so many once-familiar creatures to disappear?

To understand how this calamity has happened, we need to go back in time. And although most of the really major changes to our countryside have occurred in the past seventy years or so, to truly comprehend the enormity of this modern-day destruction we need to rewind the clock 5,000 years. Back to that anonymous early farmer, sharpening his flint axe on the hard, grey stone, before setting forth to chop down the trees that once covered these downlands.

❀

IT WOULD HAVE taken a very long period – several of these first settlers' brief and gruelling lifetimes – to make any significant change to this place; to begin to transform it from a closed, wooded landscape into an open, grassy one. As the forests disappeared, so the underlying shapes of the hillsides gradually became exposed: gentle, rounded, grassy slopes rising up above the surrounding lowlands. And as generation succeeded generation, the view gradually changed to something not all that different from the one we see today.

At Avebury, on the edge of the Marlborough Downs, these early settlers built a stone circle – the largest in Europe. Although not as famous as its neighbour Stonehenge, the Avebury circle is equally impressive; more so, perhaps, for being right by the main road that runs through the village, so that as it comes into view you are suddenly, and unexpectedly, pitched thousands of years back in time.

Many centuries later, they cut through the grass and topsoil of these hills to reveal the chalk below, creating some of the region's most famous landmarks. So on a Dorset hillside above the village of Cerne Abbas, a naked man wields a fearsome club almost as long as he is tall, complemented by his huge (and magnificently erect) penis. Further to the north-east, on the edge of Salisbury Plain, is the more wholesome – and much more recent – chalk carving of the White Horse at Westbury.

These monuments and carvings are evidence of the continued human occupation of this area over thousands of years. It was these early settlers who also shaped the wildlife of this newly changed landscape. Although we have no written records from this period, we can assume that many species that would have been rare and localised until the forests were cleared were then able to take advantage of this new habitat, extending their range and increasing in numbers to become some of our commonest plants and animals.

As well as wild flowers and their accompanying chalkland butterflies, many birds such as the rook and the skylark would have benefited from the clearance of the forests. Mammals would have thrived too: the rabbit, introduced by the Romans, and the brown hare, often thought of as a native species but also brought here from abroad, probably by the Romans' Iron Age forebears, soon became common residents of this new landscape.

When Britain was largely covered with trees, these birds and mammals would have been confined to the few areas of open land which suited their lifestyle: clifftops, the edges of higher ground, and any larger clearings within the woods and forests themselves. But gradually, as the trees were cut down and open grassland and crops began to dominate, they would have gained the upper hand on their woodland counterparts. For what we now think of as 'farmland species', the next few thousand years was a golden age, as they lived and thrived right alongside their human neighbours.

❀

UNFORTUNATELY, FOR MOST of our human history on these islands we have very little evidence of the status of these, or indeed of any of our wild creatures. Only in the seventeenth and eighteenth centuries, when visionary observers such as the Cambridge botanist John Ray and the Hampshire parson-naturalist Gilbert White began to keep detailed notes and records, do we begin to get an understanding of the relative abundance of different species.

Yet there is another way to know how common a plant or animal must have been in the distant past: by examining any names (including folk names) that have survived to the present day. The premise behind this theory is simple: rare creatures were hardly ever seen or noticed by most people, and so never acquired common names. Thus birds such as the avocet and the red-necked phalarope – both scarce and limited in range – were named in the seventeenth and eighteenth centuries by professional ornithologists. But common and widespread creatures had been given their names long before then by ordinary people, and in most cases had also been granted a series of alternative folk names, varying from place to place up and down the country.

Take that characteristic bird of the open countryside, the skylark. Originally simply known as the 'lark' (the prefix 'skie' was added in 1678 by John Ray), this once-ubiquitous open-country bird has over the centuries garnered a range of epithets, including laverock, heaven's hen, skyflapper and rising-lark. Both the official and folk names reflect the bird's amazing ability to sing while hanging in the air for what seems like hours on end; an ability so perfectly evoked in the opening lines of Victorian poet George Meredith's 'The Lark Ascending':

> He rises and begins to round,
> He drops the silver chain of sound
> Of many links without a break,
> In chirrup, whistle, slur and shake,
> All intervolv'd and spreading wide,

Like water-dimples down a tide
Where ripple ripple overcurls
And eddy into eddy whirls . . .

This familiar bird is also embedded in our day-to-day language: we say of someone that they 'sing like a lark'; we talk about an early riser as being 'up with the lark', and our grandparents' generation used to talk about 'larking about', though this now appears to have gone out of fashion.

This wide range of names and phrases applied to the bird and its behaviour tells us that the skylark would have been familiar to everyone who lived and worked in the open countryside. The same is true of other species with similarly 'basic' names such as the rook (named after its call), the whitethroat (from its appearance), the yellowhammer (from its colour – 'ammer' is an old German word meaning 'bunting'), the corn bunting (from its habitat) and the linnet (from its food – referring to the bird's liking for the seeds of flax).

The populations of these birds – and the various mammals, insects and wild flowers associated with this 'new' countryside – would have remained fairly constant over time. Certainly until the Second World War these species could be found across vast swathes of lowland Britain, wherever the land was farmed in a traditional way – which was more or less everywhere.

That's not to say that things never altered during this long period of time. One of the most dramatic changes happened in just a few decades at the end of the eighteenth and start of the nineteenth centuries, when the Enclosure Acts transformed Britain's lowland landscape for ever.

Enclosure changed the face of the countryside by encouraging the planting of hedges, which obliterated the previous system of open strip fields radiating out from a village, and created smaller, enclosed plots of land bounded by hedgerows. By allowing private landowners to separate their holdings from one another's, it also produced the familiar 'patchwork quilt' of fields we know today.

Not everyone welcomed this change: the poet John Clare, whose home on the edge of the Northamptonshire Fens was transformed out of all recognition by enclosure, was devastated by the changes to familiar landmarks. In his poem 'The Flitting' he wrote movingly of his sense of disorientation as the landscape he had known since childhood was utterly transformed in just a few years:

> [. . .], and so I seem
> Alone and in a stranger scene,
> Far, far from spots my heart esteems,
> The closen with their ancient green,
> Heaths, woods, and pastures, sunny streams.
> The hawthorns here were hung with may,
> But still they seem in deader green,

The sun een seems to lose its way
Nor knows the quarter it is in.

Devastating as the changes were for Clare and his
fellow farm labourers, the effects on wildlife were not so
serious. For although the hemming-in of fields and the
move towards more organised agriculture might have
affected some creatures of open ground, this was more than
compensated for by the new hedgerows where birds could
nest, insects feed and small mammals find a home. And
once the disruption was over, the countryside returned to
some kind of equilibrium, in which most of our familiar
farmland species continued to thrive. A century later, this
patchwork quilt of fields and hedgerows had come to be
regarded as the traditional English rural landscape.

By then, the romantic view of rural Britain had become
so familiar – not least through a series of novels by early-
twentieth-century writers such as Mary Webb – that the
journalist Stella Gibbons was able to parody the genre
mercilessly in her classic satire *Cold Comfort Farm* (1932).
In the novel, the young but determined Flora Poste seeks
to improve the lives of her cousins, the Starkadders, on
their Sussex farm:

After another minute Reuben brought forth the
following sentence: 'I ha' scranleted two hundred
furrows come five o'clock down i' the bute.' It was a
difficult remark, Flora felt, to which to reply.

23

But it was the purple prose used to describe the countryside around the farm – helpfully marked by the author using a rating system of one, two or three stars – that would have been instantly recognisable to the contemporary readers of *Cold Comfort Farm*. And as the book's final sentence suggests, not only would those readers have recognised this portrayal of rural England; they would also have assumed that it would continue into the foreseeable future.

> She glanced upwards for a second at the soft blue vault of the midsummer night sky. Not a cloud misted its solemn depths. Tomorrow would be a beautiful day.

Less than a decade later, that beautiful day was well and truly over. Britain's farmed countryside had undergone a transformation greater than any it had ever experienced: more dramatic than enclosure, and bigger, even, than the original clearing of the woods and forests. And it happened virtually overnight.

❁

THE OUTBREAK OF the Second World War in September 1939 appears to have caught the authorities unawares, perhaps because until the last moment they hoped the policy of appeasement would bear fruit. This, along with the very real threat of invasion by sea, meant that growing our own food became the top priority for the wartime government. Food rationing was swiftly introduced, but there were still almost 50 million hungry mouths to feed, and the newly created Ministry of Food was charged with that task.

For the countryside – and in particular the lowland countryside of southern and eastern England – the resulting transformation was sudden and extreme. Precious, complex habitats, which had evolved over hundreds, sometimes thousands of years, were simply destroyed.

Hay meadows, chalk grasslands and rough pastures were ploughed and planted with crops. Farm ponds and fens were drained, hedgerows grubbed up, and woods and copses bulldozed, to maximise the land available to grow crops and raise livestock.

The slogan 'Dig for Victory' and the recruitment of thousands of Land Girls lent the campaign a jaunty, positive air; and it cannot be denied that these measures made a huge contribution to the war effort, perhaps even helping to tip the balance between winning and losing.

But for the wildlife that depended on these ancient, complex habitats, the changes were, quite simply, a disaster. Once ploughed up and planted with crops, a hay meadow or hedgerow cannot be restored to its original state; the ecological complexity, evolved over decades or even centuries, is simply impossible for us to reproduce. So although this drastic action was necessary to feed the nation at a time of war, these precious places – and much of their wildlife – were gone for ever.

When the war was finally over, things might have been expected to return to normal. But they did not – indeed could not – for several very good reasons. First, the food shortages continued; indeed, in some ways they got worse. The effort of winning the war had almost bankrupted Britain, and the country was in no position to let up on producing as much food as possible. Food rationing continued for a further nine years – three years longer than the duration of the war itself – only coming to an end in 1954.

But another, more sinister factor dealt the final blow for Britain's traditional lowland countryside. A combination of economic development and scientific breakthroughs led to the rapid and wholesale adoption of 'chemical farming': the use of newly created nitrate fertilisers to increase yields of crops.

At the same time, the scientists also produced a whole new range of pesticides and herbicides, which were sprayed over fields to kill off insects and weeds. Using this chemical armoury enabled farmers to squeeze even more productivity out of each precious acre of land, and feed Britain's rapidly growing post-war population.

For politicians, farmers and consumers alike, this must have seemed like the answer to their prayers. The government would be able to feed the nation and reduce expensive imports; the farmers would be able produce more food, which they could sell at a handsome profit;

and the 'housewife' (as this new breed of consumer was soon dubbed) would be able to get cheaper food.

As we now know to our cost, the new scheme worked so well that it led to a complete shift in the way we produce, buy and consume food. Whereas our grandparents bought just what they needed, day by day, from the butcher, baker, greengrocer and so on, within a couple of generations we were buying weekly, in bulk, at out-of-town supermarkets. Whereas they abhorred waste, and regularly made meals with 'leftovers', we think nothing of throwing away millions of tonnes of food, worth billions of pounds, every year. And whereas they spent a huge proportion – up to one third – of their meagre incomes on food, today we spend less than one eighth.

But in other ways, the new style of farming hasn't worked at all. Farmers have produced higher and higher yields, but this has driven prices down so far that many struggle to make a profit. They have been forced to completely change the way they farm: low profit margins and high labour costs mean they must do the vast majority of the work themselves; even at their low wages, farm workers are often too expensive to employ.

To maximise yields, they are in hock to the major chemical companies, without whom they simply cannot produce the food at the price they will be paid. And they have had to choose between different types of farming: 'mixed farms', raising livestock as well as growing crops, have now virtually disappeared; instead farmers are forced to specialise in either arable or pastoral farming. Thus our countryside is now divided between the wetter west, where livestock dominates, and the drier east, where arable farming rules.

❀

NOT SURPRISINGLY, THIS change in the way we farm the land continues to have a devastating effect on our wildlife. In 2013 an alliance of twenty-five environmental organisations produced the *State of Nature* report, launched by Sir David Attenborough. The report revealed that of just over 3,000 species surveyed, 60 per cent have decreased, and almost one third have decreased strongly. Not surprisingly, given the prominence of farming, creatures of the open countryside featured prominently, with more than one third of the 1,064 species dependent on farmland declining strongly, especially birds, butterflies and wild flowers.

The report firmly put the blame for these declines on changes in the way Britain's countryside is managed, especially those designed to boost productivity. It also pointed out that despite the introduction of 'agri-environment schemes' specifically designed to boost wildlife, most farmland species have failed to recover from the declines of recent decades.

Cynics might dismiss this as a bunch of greenies crying wolf, were it not for the fact that the government's own research has come to exactly the same conclusion.

A report from DEFRA (also in 2013) on wild-bird populations in the UK revealed that farmland birds have declined faster and further than any other group, and that even though the largest decline occurred between the late 1970s and early 1990s, there has been a further major fall in numbers during the past decade.

The government's report concluded that many of these declines have been caused by the intensification of farming, including the loss of mixed farming, a move from spring to autumn sowing of arable crops, a switch from making hay to producing silage (fermented grass used to feed livestock), increased use of pesticides and fertilisers, and the removal of hedgerows – all of which are proven to be detrimental to wildlife.

Habitat loss is only one problem. Another is the constant refinement of chemical weapons used to wage war against any insect or invertebrate 'pests' that might reduce the yield of arable crops. One group of these, the neonicotinoids, has recently become the subject of controversy and debate: do these chemicals, as the manufacturers suggest, target pests so efficiently that they cause little or no harm to benevolent insects such as butterflies and bumblebees; or are they, as the evidence now appears to show, lethal both to those insects, dramatically reducing their numbers, and to the birds that eat seeds treated with them?

As the decline in farmland wildlife continues – despite many schemes to restore lost habitat and provide wild creatures with homes – it seems more and more likely that when we use these lethal pesticides to kill off billions of insects, we also kill off the insect-eaters; by removing the essential food supply these birds and mammals need to feed their young. These chemicals also stay around for a very long time, contaminating soils and entering watercourses such as ditches, streams and rivers.

❁

THE NATIONAL FARMERS' Union (NFU) would have us believe that nothing is wrong. As their 2015 General Election Manifesto proclaims, 'UK farmers and growers are proud of the environmental improvements made over the past twenty-five years.'

But the reality on the ground clearly contradicts this view. Those of us who have witnessed these catastrophic declines within our own lifetimes know that our farmland wildlife is declining as never before. And now both independent and government reports have confirmed this.

What is abundantly clear is that the system of farming in Britain is broken. True, some people do benefit: supermarkets and their shareholders; a handful of very rich landowners, foreign oligarchs and pension funds, who between them own vast swathes of Britain's farmland; and of course the rest of us – at least anyone who buys cheap food. That means virtually everyone.

Those who lose out include most farmers, many of whom struggle to make a living, as the price they receive for their produce is forced lower and lower by predatory wholesalers and supermarkets. Sometimes, as in the case of milk, the price per litre paid to the farmer is actually less than the cost it takes to produce. But the biggest losers are the wild creatures that used to thrive in our fields and meadows; and the millions of Britons who, whether they live in the cities or the countryside, care deeply about the natural world.

We urgently need to find another way of farming: a way that would make room for wildlife while still producing the food we need – albeit at prices that reflect the effort that goes into this process, and reward the farmers properly for all their hard work.

Opponents claim that this would cost too much money: reduced yields would mean less income for the hard-pressed farmers, which would tip them over the edge into economic ruin, force prices up in the shops and lead to food shortages and empty shelves in the supermarkets.

That might be true if Britain's farming system were a genuinely free market, but of course it isn't. It is a dependency culture, corrupted by a system of taxpayers' handouts that makes social-security benefit cheats look like rank amateurs; a system that rewards the bigger, richer farmers and penalises the smaller, poorer ones, by forcing down the prices they get for their produce; and a system that seems expressly designed to be bad for Britain's wildlife and the wider countryside.

This system, which has now been running in one form or another for almost seven decades, depends on vast subsidies to keep it afloat: £3 billion every year – roughly £50 for every man, woman and child in the UK. So a typical 'hard-working family', to use a phrase beloved of our politicians, pays Britain's farmers £4 a week – £200 a year.

What is most pernicious about this continued subsidy is that while in the past it was at least vaguely related to the way each recipient farmed their land, under the new Basic Payment Scheme the money each landowner receives is entirely dependent on the area of land they own. So the more land they have, the more of our money they get – about £200 per hectare, every single year.

Roughly 100,000 people claim farm subsidies. So on average, each should receive £30,000 a year; but given that there is a huge disparity in size between small family farms and large estates, this of course varies hugely. Indeed, many of the larger landowners – including several current and former government ministers – have over the past decade been given millions of pounds in taxpayer-funded subsidies. But much of this doesn't go to the people who actually farm the land. That's because much of Britain's farmland, which includes grouse moors and shooting estates as well as arable and livestock farms, is worked by tenants, but owned by huge corporations and wealthy foreign individuals. Environmentalist George

Monbiot has aptly described the latter as 'the world's most successful benefit tourists'.

It doesn't have to be like this. We could simply shift these subsidies so that they reward farmers who are doing their best – against the odds, and with little or no encouragement from the NFU – to farm in a more wildlife-friendly way. Without paying out a single penny more in taxpayers' cash, we could not only help wildlife but also create a host of wider environmental benefits, from preventing floods to reducing greenhouse-gas emissions. We'd have a more attractive, cleaner and much more accessible countryside. And it goes without saying that we would have a lot more wildlife.

❀

THE GOOD NEWS – and there is not much good news out there – is that a substantial minority of farmers agrees with the view that farming must actively seek to make room for wildlife. Living and working on the land, they have grown to love the wild creatures they come across, and to value a rich and diverse landscape. Some, indeed, have gone one step further: ensuring that they farm in a wildlife-friendly way, even if this may mean sacrificing a small proportion of their profits to do so.

One of these was – until he retired from farming a few years ago – Chris Knights. Norfolk born and bred, with the soft local burr and idiosyncratic view of the world often found in this corner of East Anglia, Chris now has plenty of time to pursue his passion for wildlife photography, travelling the world to obtain stunning shots of birds and other wild creatures.

But his fascination with wildlife never distracted him from the important business of making a living from farming, working hard to produce crops on his land to supply our shops and supermarkets, and put food on our dinner tables.

When I entered Chris's farmyard for the first time, on a hot July afternoon more than a decade ago, initial appearances were deceptive. Bits and pieces of old machinery covered with weeds might have led me to assume – quite wrongly – that this was no longer a working farm. The impression that things had been benignly neglected was deliberate: Chris never believed in clearing up too much, for a messy farmyard is always better for wildlife than a tidy one. And the place was simply teeming with birds: a blackbird with its bill crammed with worms to take back to its hungry brood of young; a pied wagtail balancing uneasily on the lichen-covered weathervane on top of the barn; house sparrows, as I expected, but also the scarcer and shyer tree sparrows; and flocks of chaffinches, linnets and goldfinches, the latter using their needle-sharp bills to extract the tiny teasel seeds from their cases.

Swallows perched on telegraph wires, twittering to one another before sallying forth to grab a tiny insect from out of the ether. House martins, looking like miniature killer whales in their smart navy-and-white plumage, grabbed beakfuls of mud to take back to their nests suspended beneath the eaves of Chris's farmhouse. And hidden in the foliage along the old brick wall of the farmhouse garden, a dunnock sat snugly incubating her clutch of five eggs, whose pale blue colour seemed to reflect the shade of the summer sky above.

Chris took me on a tour of the farm in his Range Rover, and I discovered just how good farmland can be for birds – when, that is, the land is managed with their welfare in mind. The native grey partridge – what Chris calls the 'English partridge' – is one of the most subtly beautiful of all our birds, as I saw for myself when we came across a pair of nervous adults accompanied by their chicks. As they hurriedly led the youngsters to safety in the long grass, I noticed the delicately mottled browns, buffs and chestnuts of their plumage, mingling with soft pearly greys to produce a very pleasing whole.

Grey partridge numbers have gone down by more than 90 per cent since 1967, and the species' breeding range has shrunk by almost half during the same period. Ironically, it mainly hangs on where the land is deliberately managed for shooting and, on some estates, because birds are artificially bred and released to maintain their numbers.

Chris still had good numbers of partridges on his land for one very simple reason: he always left the fringes of the fields alone, so that daisies, docks, mayweeds and thistles could thrive. This created plenty of cover for the nesting birds, and attracted insects on which the chicks then fed.

But Chris had saved his star bird until the very end of our tour. We walked slowly by a strip of maize planted along the edge of a ploughed field, and as we did so a long-legged bird rose slowly from the ground, took a couple of steps forward, and then melted back into the crops, just out of view.

It was a stone-curlew, surely one of Britain's most bizarre birds. Technically it is a wader, though I have never seen one anywhere near water, let alone wading. Like the partridges it evolved to live on semi-natural grasslands, and now ekes out a precarious existence on a few areas of farmland in East Anglia and the chalk downlands of southern England, wherever landowners are sympathetic to its complex needs.

As with the partridges and farmyard songbirds, the stone-curlews are only here because Chris created the habitat for them. Instead of the wall-to-wall crops found on most other farms in this area – and indeed on most arable farms in Britain – Chris deliberately made room for species such as the stone-curlew to thrive. It's a species he has known well since he was a teenager – he recalls taking his very first photos of this enigmatic bird back in the late 1950s.

These birds are simply the visible tip of a much greater range of wild creatures: they are only here because of the wild flowers and insects, which in turn encourage small mammals, most of which we never see, but which help support a range of larger predators such as owls and raptors.

For Chris, having these creatures on his land is what has made his life as a farmer worthwhile: he may have lost a tiny percentage of his profit, but in his view that has been more than compensated for by the joy and pleasure he has always gained from watching the wild creatures with which he shares this little corner of Norfolk.

❀

ANOTHER OF EAST Anglia's wildlife-friendly farmers lives not amongst the gently rolling hills of west Norfolk, but on the stark flatlands of Lincolnshire, in what was once the Fens. Hundreds of years ago this was home to some of the greatest wildlife spectacles Britain has ever seen: awash with wetland birds, butterflies and a host of other wild creatures. But as Britain's population grew, such a paradise could not last. From the Middle Ages onwards, concerted efforts were made to remove the water, turning the Fens into land that could be ploughed and planted with crops, or used to graze animals.

This area of East Anglia has become the breadbasket of Britain, where intensive farming has reached its logical zenith. So as I drove north-westwards, circling the edge of the Wash and entering this flat, bleak landscape with its wide-open fields and big skies, it was all too easy to become depressed by the wildlife I was seeing – or rather, by the almost complete lack of it.

The odd crow flapped lazily across a field of wheat or barley, and small flocks of gulls gathered along the roadsides; but otherwise the absence of wild creatures was increasingly apparent. The Ry Cooder track playing on my car stereo – all shivering slide guitar and bottleneck rattling the strings – seemed strangely appropriate to this flat, unbroken landscape of big skies and heat haze on the horizon. If I half-closed my eyes, I could be driving across the vast prairies of the midwestern states of the USA, rather than rural East Anglia.

I stopped in a lay-by and got out of the car, being careful to avoid a juggernaut thundering along the carriageway towards the west. As the sound faded away, I cupped my ears and listened to . . . nothing. Not a sound. Not the tuneful song of the skylark or the discordant jangling of the corn bunting. Not the croak of a partridge hidden in the crops, or the buzzing of bumblebees as they foraged in the adjacent field.

I got back into the car, turned up the stereo, and headed from Norfolk into Lincolnshire. Then, on the edge of the village of Deeping St Nicholas, the view began to change; becoming less uniform, less rigid, and a little messier at the edges. Pulling over once again, I opened the car window and to my joy I heard a chorus of skylarks – the first I had come across for many miles.

From a deep dyke forming a watery border between the field and the road, an excitable, chattering sound indicated a hidden sedge warbler, presumably nesting in the thick vegetation along the banks. It was swiftly answered by the more rhythmic, measured tones of its cousin the reed warbler. In the distance, three species of buntings chorused away: corn bunting, sounding like the rattling of a bunch of keys; yellowhammers, with their 'little-bit-of-bread-and-no-cheeeese' song; and from a crop of oilseed rape, a reed bunting, sounding rather like a bored sound engineer checking out his PA system before a gig: 'one . . . two . . . testing . . .'

I could almost begin to imagine what this wider landscape might have sounded like before drainage and industrial agriculture transformed it into the food factory we see today. But it doesn't take much to make room for wildlife. A strip of weeds here, a stand of reeds alongside a dyke there, are all birds, bees and butterflies need to make a home.

This is Vine House Farm. The reason so many birds live here is because the man who farms this land, Nicholas Watts, is also a lifelong ornithologist. Nicholas comes from a long line of farmers: his great-grandfather moved here in 1883, and four generations of the Watts family – including Nicholas and his three daughters – have been born and raised here. So he has always felt a deep connection with this corner of Lincolnshire, especially with its birds and other wildlife.

One morning more than thirty years ago, Nicholas set out with a pen and a map to systematically record the birds breeding on his farm, something he has continued to do every year since. But as time went by, he began to notice that the classic birds of arable farmland – especially skylarks and corn buntings – were beginning to decline, so he decided to give them a helping hand by putting out large quantities of seed in his farmyards.

This proved so successful that he held an open day, inviting his neighbours and any passers-by to drop in and see the birds for themselves. Some of the visitors asked if he sold birdseed, so he packaged some up for them, giving the proceeds to the Lincolnshire Wildlife Trust. Thus, completely by accident, he realised he might have a business opportunity that would benefit both him and the birds.

Today Nicholas – together with his daughter Lucy and son-in-law Robert – now has more than 160 hectares (over 400 acres) devoted entirely to growing bird food: not just sunflowers, but also red and white millet, canary seed, oats, wheat and oilseed rape. Vine House Farm Bird Food is now a thriving commercial business, selling birdseed by mail order all over the country.

But Nicholas didn't stop there. Year after year, he has taken steps to improve the habitat available for wildlife. First, he persuaded the local drainage board only to cut the vegetation along the dykes on alternate sides each year, and not until late autumn, thus preserving a vital habitat for species such as those sedge and reed warblers

I heard on my way to the farm, along with even scarcer species such as yellow wagtails. He also keeps a 2-metre strip along the margins of each field free from crops; which may not sound much, but with 25 kilometres of field margins this adds up to 50,000 square metres – 5 hectares – of extra wildlife habitat.

Nicholas has planted more than 6 kilometres of hedgerow in the past ten years, along with three woodland spinneys, 8 hectares of wild-flower meadows, and a series of farm ponds. These support a wide variety of wetland birds including oystercatchers and fifty pairs of common terns, whose harsh calls echo around the Lincolnshire landscape on spring and summer days, bringing a flavour of the seaside far inland.

This isn't just on his own farm: he has also encouraged his neighbours to keep, rather than demolish, redundant barns and other farm buildings, and as a result in 2014 twenty pairs of barn owls nested in the area – the best year ever. Overall, almost all the farmland species declining locally as well as nationally are now on the increase here.

Ironically, it could so easily have been very different. At the time when Nicholas started his bird-food business, he faced intense pressure to make his farm not more wildlife friendly, but less. Falling prices paid by the big supermarkets to farmers were forcing many of his neighbours to fill in their dykes to create much larger fields, and to maximise yields by removing any vegetation along the field margins. By deliberately taking a different path, and yet still making a healthy profit through his birdseed and farm business, he has proved that you don't need to exclude wildlife to farm successfully, even in the modern age.

For all the hard work he has done to draw attention to the plight of farmland birds and ways to improve their fortunes, Nicholas has deservedly won a number of honours, including the MBE in 2006, and in 2013 the prestigious RSPB Nature of Farming award.

❀

CHRIS KNIGHTS AND Nicholas Watts are just two of an increasing number of far-sighted farmers who have decided not to go down the road of producing food at any cost, but to do so in a way that makes room for wildlife. So why can't the majority of Britain's farmers join them, to work their land in a sustainable, wildlife-friendly way? Unless they do so, the declines in our wildlife are set to continue.

Maybe there is a way to change the way we farm – not just through individual farmers, but on a far bigger scale. For, as we are discovering in all areas of nature conservation, we really do need to think big.

Back on the Marlborough Downs, 5,000 years after those early farmers first began the task of turning this land from forest into farmland, that's exactly what is happening. Here a group of more than forty farmers –

some of whom own vast estates, while others run small family farms – have joined forces to make the place better for wildlife. Together they own more than 10,000 hectares – about 40 square miles – stretching from the outskirts of Swindon in the north to the ancient settlement of Avebury in the south. So as I walk westwards along the Ridgeway, virtually the whole of the land I can see, all the way to the horizon in every direction, is under their stewardship.

These men and women are driven by a combination of hard work, determination and a good dollop of bloody-mindedness. They have also sought help and advice from outside experts, along with a chunk of money from the government, as part of a pilot scheme known as a Nature Improvement Area (NIA).

They are doing this because although they want to produce food and make a living, they recognise – as do, in my experience, most farmers – that nature has an essential part to play in our agricultural landscape. They believe that the British countryside without wildlife would, to all intents and purposes, cease to be the British countryside: in the words of ornithologist Jeremy Mynott, it would become the 'non-urban green space'.

These people are not idealistic hippies, 'hobby farmers' or millionaire former pop stars who can afford to lose money in order to salve their social conscience; they are pragmatic, hard-headed businessmen and -women. When asked what is their main purpose in life, they will say that it is to produce food, to sell to consumers to help feed the nation, and in turn enable them to support their own families – both now and in the future. They see themselves, quite rightly, as the temporary caretakers of the land, and know that just as they benefited from the hard work and tough decisions taken by their forebears, so their own descendants will only be able to continue to live and work here if they manage the land properly.

Above all, they care deeply about the environment – which is not surprising, really, as they spend the vast majority of their lives here. David White is one of the driving forces behind this project, and his deep connection with this place is obvious the moment I meet him. He is the fourth generation of his family to have farmed this corner of Wiltshire – his son, who now does much of the day-to-day running of the farm, is the fifth, and already there are grandchildren being lined up to follow him.

David greets me outside his beautiful fifteenth-century farmhouse with characteristic bonhomie. Along with his home and family, he has another passion that he is eager to share with me: photographing the wild creatures that live on his land. He proudly shows me his portfolio of pictures: stunning images of a kestrel grappling with a barn owl in flight, a roe deer peeping shyly out of a field of golden barley, and a pair of birds so rare I cannot even name them here, but which are amongst the scarcest breeding birds in Britain. I'm eager to see this wildlife for myself so, climbing into David's battered and muddy

Land Rover, we head out of the farmyard, along the road and onto the farm itself.

As we toil up the hill towards the top of the ridge, small birds flit in and out of the hedgerow: linnets, their flickering wings glinting in the midday sun, and yellowhammers, the males proudly showing off their canary-coloured heads. A grey partridge runs rapidly across the track, swiftly followed by another, while in the distance I can hear the jangling song of a corn bunting, serenading his harem of females.

Almost all of these are absent from my own corner of the countryside, an hour or so's drive down the road in Somerset. Yet here they are thriving; and they're not the only ones. Hares sprint along field boundaries before diving for cover. Roe deer pop their heads up from the middle of the barley crop, before bounding off into the distance on spring-loaded legs. And bumblebees and butterflies float over the hedgerows, before descending to feed on nectar-rich wild flowers, whose heady scent fills the summer's air.

This wonderful array of wildlife isn't here by accident. David and his fellow farmers have encouraged it, nurtured it and enabled it to thrive by a carefully planned strategy of extending existing habitats, creating new ones, and joining them all together in a way that encourages a greater range and number of plants and animals.

We pull up at the edge of a field and David introduces me to Matt Prior, a local birder who has devoted countless hours to studying the lives of the tree sparrow, the scarcer and less familiar cousin of the humble house sparrow. I can recall watching tree sparrows in Bushy Park on the western outskirts of London back in the 1970s, but they are long gone from there; and indeed from much of the rest of Britain, having declined hugely during the closing decades of the twentieth century. Although numbers have slowly risen since then, there is still a very long way to go until this unassuming bird returns to many of its former haunts.

We are standing at the corner of a field with a thick hawthorn hedgerow running alongside it, and after a few moments I notice a small flock of birds amongst the dense, prickly foliage. Each superficially resembles the more familiar house sparrow, with the same squat shape, buffish-grey underparts and streaky black-and-chestnut back and wings. But they appear somehow neater, with a bright white face set off with a small black spot behind and below the eye, and a rich, chestnut-coloured cap.

Matt tells me that just as we humans have certain very specific requirements when we are looking for a place to live, so do tree sparrows. Indeed, their habits are so like ours – colonial, sociable and at times rather fussy – that we are able to draw an analogy between life for the local people in this area of rural Britain, and what kind of 'des res' the sparrows require: a tree-sparrow village, as Matt calls it.

Tree sparrows are sedentary birds, with the youngsters from last year's brood sticking close to where they were born and raised, so we need to create 'starter homes' close to existing colonies. Matt does so by providing specially made nest boxes, ideal for the youngsters to move straight into the year after they fledge.

Like us, tree sparrows need to feel safe and secure, especially when bringing up a family. So dense prickly scrub like this stand of hawthorns is ideal, enabling them to avoid predators such as roving sparrowhawks, always on the lookout for an easy meal. They also need a convenient supply of food – 'a village shop', if you like – so the farmers here have planted seed mixes along the edges of their fields. These provide plenty of seeds in autumn and winter, and nectar-rich wild flowers to attract insects during the spring and summer.

Finally, for tree sparrows – and indeed for all farmland wildlife – corridors are vital: as stepping stones that enable them to travel safely from one area to another, and gradually expand their range. So the farmers have planted mile after mile of hedgerows – the bird equivalent of country lanes, with routes in and out of their 'village'.

It is this kind of far-sighted yet simple and practical approach that has enabled these farmers on the Marlborough Downs to boost both the quality and quantity of wildlife found on their farms, while continuing to produce food and make a profit. Elsewhere, farms may provide one or two of the things wild creatures need: hedgerows, perhaps, or a farm pond; but lack other fundamental requirements such as nectar-rich flowers attracting insects in summer, or seeds and grains on which birds and mammals can feed in winter.

Here the 'joined-up approach' really does work. First, the farmers find out exactly what each species needs at each point in its complex lifecycle, and then they provide it. They do so on a landscape-wide scale, so that, instead of tiny, isolated outposts into which the wildlife must squeeze, there are thriving, varied and connected networks of habitat supporting a complex range of different plants and animals throughout the year.

This is just one small example of the work these farmers are doing to attract and keep wildlife. They are also creating dew ponds along the top of the ridge where birds and mammals can drink and bathe, planting tens of thousands of trees to create a more varied and visually attractive landscape, and creating wild-flower corridors to extend the chalk grassland habitat here on the Downs.

It's hard to say how much it has cost to bring the wildlife back here, because we cannot put a price on the efforts of the individual farmers, their families, the professional conservationists and the many volunteers who give up so much of their valuable time to make this scheme work.

But we do know that the whole project has cost just £600,000 of taxpayers' money spread over three years, in addition to the payments the farmers were already receiving from agri-environment schemes. £200,000 a year may sound a lot, until you consider that it is a mere 0.007

per cent of the £3 billion we give in subsidies each year to Britain's farmers, most of which produces absolutely no benefit at all for our countryside or its wildlife.

Put another way, of the taxes we all give to support Britain's agricultural industry, each of us has paid just one third of one penny towards the Marlborough Downs scheme. For what these farmers have given back to our natural heritage, landscape and countryside, that's pretty good value.

Ultimately, of course, farming in Britain will only change because the farmers want it to. And as the people on the Marlborough Downs like to point out, their scheme has only worked because the impetus came from the bottom up. Because all the farmers here bought into the project, and put in so much of their time to make it succeed, they feel a real sense of ownership. This personal connection means that in the longer term, when the government money runs out, wildlife-friendly farming will continue to thrive here. And the scheme has had other, unexpected benefits: allowing people to get to know their neighbours, creating a more cohesive sense of community, and putting the Marlborough Downs firmly on the map.

❀

THESE FARMERS HAVE in common a deep passion for wildlife, and for the land they and the wild creatures share: the countryside. They have turned this passion into practical ways of helping nature; while never forgetting that their primary aim is to provide enough food for the consumer – you and me. They have all gone the extra mile, showing their neighbours, rural communities up and down the country and organisations such as the NFU that with a little effort, thought and creativity intensive farming can indeed coexist with nature, feeding the nation while keeping our natural heritage alive.

Sadly, they are still in a minority. Most farmers – however much they care for the countryside and its wildlife – close their eyes to the harsh reality of what their way of life is doing: driving out nature until there is nothing left behind. Given the other pressures they face, this is perhaps understandable; yet if we cannot persuade them to change their ways, and give them practical help to do so, our countryside and its wildlife are ultimately doomed.

Despite all the evidence to the contrary, many people continue to believe that our wildlife is safe in the hands of farmers. This might be because we are constantly fed an outdated view of what farming actually is – a benevolent, caring stewardship of the countryside, as opposed to the hard-nosed industry it has become.

And we continue to pay farmers huge amounts of taxpayers' money, with very little return for our wildlife. This isn't because the agricultural sector is a key employer – the number of people actually working on the land, even in rural communities, is negligible. Nor is agriculture a significant contributor to the total economy, being dwarfed by financial services and manufacturing.

More and more, Britain's farming industry is coming to resemble the mining industry in the 1970s: a fiercely tribal group of proud, hard-working people led by a small band of inflexible ideologues, fundamentally out of touch with both public opinion and the needs of a rapidly changing world.

Millions of people – many living in towns and cities, others in the countryside – are members of conservation organisations: the 1 million members of the RSPB, the 800,000 members of the 47 Wildlife Trusts, and the 4.5 million members of the National Trust. Yet a relatively small minority – the 100,000 members of the Countryside Alliance and the 85,000 members of the NFU – currently dictate what happens in the farmed countryside, a place in which, whether they like it or not, we all have a stake.

The members – and the leaders – of those nature-conservation organisations must demand that they too are able to have a say in the way our countryside is managed. Its future is far too important to be left in the hands of those with a vested interest in preserving the status quo. And we must continue to ask the crucial question to governments, the food industry, supermarkets, the farmers' union and many of the farmers themselves: Why do you persist in following the same path, when it is so clearly unsustainable?

The farmers I have had the privilege to get to know are doing an incredible job for farming and wildlife, as well as for their local communities and the wider countryside. Instead of marginalising or ignoring them, we should place them at centre stage, rolling out the things they have done all across the farmed landscape of Britain. Then we would have the best of both worlds: a healthy supply of food and a place for Britain's farmland wildlife.

It seems to me that we have a simple choice. We can continue to farm unsustainably, with little or no regard for nature, to supply the ever-growing demand for cheap food. Or we can choose an alternative path, creating a way of farming which combines the best of the modern and the traditional, which is both sustainable and profitable, and which puts people, places and wildlife at its very heart. This is not about preserving the landscape in aspic, but instead – following in the 5,000-year-old tradition of change wrought by human hand – managing it to shape something that benefits us all. After all, we created this landscape; so we can change it for the better.

✿

BACK ON THE Marlborough Downs, as dusk falls, a barn owl takes to the wing, a pale, ghostly shape floating low and silent in the evening air. It sweeps on soft, rounded wings across the hedgerow, and above the wild flowers and long, swaying grasses growing along the margin of the barley field.

Hearing a rustle in the grass below it turns, folds its wings and drops down onto an unsuspecting vole. Moments later it rises back up into the air, its talons gripping its prey, and heads off to feed its hungry chicks. Here, at least, Britain's farmland wildlife is being given a second chance.

2

The Wild Wood

Woods and Forests

When the oak is felled the whole forest echoes with its fall, but a hundred acorns are sown in silence by an unnoticed breeze.

Thomas Carlyle

MY FRIEND AND colleague, the wildlife sound recordist Gary Moore, has described the experience of listening to the dawn chorus as 'audio yoga'. And it's certainly true that when you listen to a performance of spring birdsong you are left feeling calmer and more relaxed than when you began.

That's why, on a surprisingly chilly May morning, I stand in the middle of an oak wood on the edge of a valley in mid-Wales, awaiting the start of what has been called the greatest free show on earth. It is still dark, and very early: at this time of year you need to be up and about before three o'clock in the morning if you want to hear the very first bird.

I shiver, and not just from the cold, but in delicious anticipation: which species will be the first to begin?

From previous experience I know that the blackbird or robin are usually the earliest singers; though in woods alongside farmland I have heard the soothing cooing of a wood pigeon, the harsh cawing of rooks, and even the distant song of a skylark, long before any of the woodland singers have begun.

But this morning it is indeed the blackbird that opens the event, his characteristically deep, measured phrases echoing around the forest clearing as they bounce off the ancient, gnarled oaks. Within minutes, more blackbird song has joined the chorus, along with the lighter, higher-pitched tune of the robin, the syncopated seesaw of the great tit, and the trill of half a dozen wrens, each trying to outdo his rivals with volume and energy.

Half an hour or so passes before the first of the returning migrants joins in. First, the metronomic two-note song of the chiffchaff; then the rapid warble of the delicate, tuneful blackcap, which sounds rather like a speeded-up blackbird; and finally the plaintive cadence of the willow warbler, notes descending the scale like a stream running down the side of a hill.

Moments later, I hear one of three species for which these western oakwoods are a temporary summer home: the silvery sound of a wood warbler. I strain to see the singer: a lemon-and-pale-green sprite perched high in the canopy, whose plumage seems to blend with the sunlit leaves in which it sits. I catch a glimpse of his pale underside as he delivers a delicate trill like a rapidly spinning coin, followed by a wistful whistling call, before he melts back into the foliage.

The wood warbler, along with the black-and-white pied flycatcher and the rufous, black-and-grey redstart, is a true long-haul traveller to our shores. All three of these migrant songbirds spend the winter well south of the Sahara in West Africa, returning here each spring to raise a family in these Welsh oak woodlands.

It is always a treat to see and hear these birds, a welcome reminder of the wonders of bird migration. Wondrous, too, how here these global travellers rub shoulders with resident birds like the blue tits, which during the whole of their brief but eventful lives may never venture more than a mile or two from the hole in the oak tree where they hatched out.

Two hours later, by the time the sun begins to filter through the leaves to create dappled patterns of light on the woodland floor, the dawn chorus has already peaked; its volume and intensity are in decline as the birds head off to find food for their rapidly growing chicks. I wander out of the wood, where the first buzzards and red kites are already rising into the sky, mewing to one another as they float high overhead.

When describing the experience of listening to a dawn chorus, it's very hard not to fall back on musical analogies. The birds are an orchestra, tuning up to perform a symphony. Or perhaps this is more like a quasi-religious experience: a choir singing to the Creator in the midst of a forest cathedral.

But for the birds themselves, their song is simply a biological imperative, whose purpose is to repel rivals, mark out territory and attract a mate. So from a scientific point of view the whole concept of 'dawn chorus' is utterly misleading. Rather than forming a coherent whole, each individual is simply singing for members of its own tribe. And instead of listening to the chorus of birdsong, they are filtering out the background noise of every other bird apart from their peers, rather as we are able to pick out a familiar voice amidst the hubbub of a crowded room.

Does being aware of this biological background to birdsong make the dawn chorus any less miraculous? Paradoxically, perhaps, I think not. Indeed for me, understanding *why* birds sing enhances the whole experience, enabling me to marvel at the incredible complexity of their lives, yet also to enjoy the feeling that this wall of sound engenders in my soul: a feeling of being totally and utterly alive.

❊

MY RESPONSE TO the dawn chorus is typical of our modern way of looking at woods and forests: as a resource for us to enjoy. Today we mostly regard them as places of leisure and recreation; places we go for a walk with the kids, enjoy mountain biking or horse riding, or simply as somewhere to escape the stresses and strains of modern life.

There's nothing wrong with all that; indeed, their ubiquity and accessibility makes woodlands one of the most popular and effective places to engage with the natural world – certainly a lot easier to gain access to than most of Britain's farmland. But ironically, the more we impose our own agenda onto these places, the more we are likely to lose touch with the way woods work, and especially how they can be best maintained for the benefit of both people and wildlife.

Our distant ancestors would have regarded woodland very differently. For them, woods and forests were places to find food and fuel, where they lived out their short, harsh and uneventful lives in what historian William Manchester memorably called 'a world lit only by fire'. So for them, that early-morning chorus of birdsong would have had a very different meaning. It was the signal that the sun would soon be up, and another day of back-breaking and repetitive toil was about to begin.

From the time the first Neolithic settlers arrived here, the landscape of these islands had slowly begun to change, as they chopped down the trees to create areas where they could grow crops and raise their livestock. However, this may not have been quite so dramatic as is often assumed: the late Oliver Rackham, doyen of woodland ecologists, challenged the prevailing theory that Britain was once an island of trees, blanketed with a layer of woods and forests from coast to coast. Instead he suggested that our woodland was always more like the African savannah than a thick forest, with sunlit clearings interspersed amongst the trees.

Nevertheless, as the human population grew, the clearing and felling continued, so that by the time of the Domesday Book only one seventh of the country was forested. This accelerated with the advent of the Industrial Revolution, when a rapidly growing population and the new market for manufactured goods meant that the demand for wood for fuel and building materials soared. Woodlands also stood in the way of development; during the nineteenth and twentieth centuries vast swathes of our forests were removed to make way for railways, roads, homes and factories, so that today only a fraction – about 2 per cent of the trees that were here originally – remains.

Those woods and forests that have survived are as complex and intricate as any city: their ancient trees the natural equivalent of antique cathedrals or modern skyscrapers, each a mighty monument to the greater whole. But those centuries of loss have been followed by decades of neglect, during which we largely left our woodlands to fend for themselves, instead of doing what our ancestors once did: managing them by coppicing and pollarding the trees to fulfil their own needs, and at the same time providing a home for wildlife. Over time, many of our woods and forests have fallen into disrepair and disuse.

Yet despite the battering they have taken over the millennia, Britain's woodlands remain – perhaps surprisingly – amongst our most fertile and productive wild places. They may take a little time to give up their secrets, yet they are also the richest natural habitat in the whole of the country, simply bursting with life – just as long as you know where to look.

From badgers to bluebells, butterflies to beetles, and woodpeckers to wrens, Britain's woods and forests are home to an extraordinary range of wild creatures. The reason is that they are a truly three-dimensional habitat: existing on every level from beneath the soil to the very top of the tree canopy. This creates a range of microhabitats where many different plants, animals and other organisms such as fungi can find a niche. A single oak tree can support hundreds of other species, from birds nesting amidst the branches, to moths laying their eggs on the undersides of the leaves; from jays and squirrels feeding on the acorns to deer browsing the foliage; and countless other insects and invertebrates.

Perhaps more than any other home for wildlife, woods and forests demonstrate the sheer complexity of a system that begins with the fungi and tree roots stretching far underground; develops through the trees themselves, the wild flowers that grow beneath them, and the insects and other invertebrates that depend on these trees and plants;

and culminates in the variety of birds and mammals that in turn depend on the seeds, fruit and insects which flourish there.

❈

ALTHOUGH OUR CONNECTION with woods and forests may not always be at the forefront of our daily lives, it is nevertheless a profound one. And when it does come to the surface, we may be surprised by its intensity. This goes some way to explain the events of October 2010, when the government announced that it would be selling off a sizeable chunk of our woodlands to help pay down the public deficit. When details of the plan to sell about half of the land under Forestry Commission ownership – totalling about 4000 square kilometres – became known, there was an immediate public outcry.

Signs proclaiming 'Hands Off Our Forests' and 'Not For Sale' sprang up all over the country, and the government was soon forced into a humiliating U-turn. The sheer emotional force of the backlash against privatisation was clear evidence, were it ever needed, of our deep emotional connection with trees, woods and forests; an emotional connection people are willing to defend with a heartfelt passion.

Yet much of this undoubtedly sincere and deeply held passion to save our woodlands from privatisation was based on an erroneous belief: that of all our landscapes, woods and forests are somehow the most 'natural'. Just as our farmed countryside has been shaped over centuries by human hands, so have Britain's woods and forests – albeit, perhaps, in a less obvious way. We might assume that forestry is somehow closer to nature than conventional farming: that all the woodsman has to do is to plant a tree, wait a couple of decades, and then come along and chop it down. But of course the whole process is far more complex. Like any crop, trees – and the woods and forests where they grow – must be carefully managed in order to provide us with the products we need.

So even though many people regard trees as holy relics, to be left untouched and uncut, the truth is that in many cases trees and forests thrive better when they are actively managed by human hand. Traditional processes such as coppicing and pollarding not only extend the life of a tree and help maintain a flourishing woodland, but also provide a regular supply of wood for the forester.

As well as benefiting trees, woods and foresters, active management of woodlands helps wildlife too. By cutting down the tree almost to ground level, leaving only a short stump from which new growth will emerge, coppicing lets light down through the canopy and onto the forest floor. Light quite literally brings life: allowing wild flowers such as bluebells and primroses to flourish, which in turn attracts a myriad of insects, providing food for woodland birds, and keeping the whole cycle going.

These patches of dappled light, where sunlight and shade gently battle one another as the sun passes across the sky, create complex microhabitats: specific conditions that are ideal for particular creatures, in a way that pure light or shade, or a dense, thick canopy of an unmanaged woodland, do not.

Two woodland butterflies – one common and widespread, the other far more rare and localised – demonstrate the benefits of having a blend of light and shade. Walk through any woodland from April to September, and you'll usually catch sight of a small brown butterfly with buffish-yellow markings on its upperwings, fluttering low above the undergrowth. This is the aptly named speckled wood, and it loves the combination of sunlight and shade you find in any well-managed woodland. Indeed, speckled woods are so attached to their tiny patch of ground that they will fight off intruders: driving off any rivals that dare to trespass onto their territory.

In a few woods in southern England, such as those that ring the cathedral city of Canterbury in Kent, you may also come across the much scarcer heath fritillary: a little jewel in orange and brown, with a chequered underwing pattern in white and orange. Unlike the speckled wood, the heath fritillary is not particularly well named; it is rarely found on open, sunlit heaths, far preferring the subtler blend of shade and sunlight found in these ancient woodlands.

The heath fritillary survives here not because these woods have been left alone, but for exactly the opposite reason: because they have been carefully managed. Regular coppicing of the trees allows a particular woodland plant, the common cow-wheat, with its dainty yellow flowers, to thrive. It is not these flowers that attract the heath fritillary, but the leaves; cow-wheat is the only plant its rather fussy caterpillars will deign to feed on. Without coppicing and clearing, the woodland glades would turn first to scrub, and then to forest; the cow-wheat would not bloom, and the heath fritillary would disappear. So perhaps, given the unsuitability of its current name, we should revert to a much older name for this butterfly: the 'woodman's follower'.

❀

GETTING THIS BALANCE right – managing our woodlands so they provide just the right suite of microhabitats for a healthy variety of plants and animals – is never easy, for new and unexpected problems often arise. One example of a species that should be thriving in southern Britain, yet whose population is currently in free fall, illustrates this.

'The muntjac and the nightingale' sounds like the title of a nonsense poem by Lewis Carroll or Edward Lear. In reality, these two species should never even have met: for the nightingale is a bird of Europe and western Asia, while the muntjac – our smallest deer – was originally confined to the densely wooded hills of south-east China and Taiwan.

That was true until the eighteenth and nineteenth centuries, which saw a rapid expansion of global travel and exploration. This was combined with a mania amongst the British aristocracy and landed gentry for bringing foreign species of birds and mammals back home, in order to 'adorn and improve' our countryside. During this period, many exotic incomers were released, mostly into the wooded parks surrounding stately homes such as Woburn Abbey in Bedfordshire. It was inevitable that some species should not only escape from their semi-captive state, but also thrive in their new surroundings. Hence we now have the Canada goose and the grey squirrel, the golden pheasant and the sika deer, and a small and rather shy creature about the size of a fox terrier: the muntjac.

I can still recall the first time I saw one. I was walking through a wood in Bedfordshire, in a fruitless search for another – now probably vanished – alien species, Lady Amherst's pheasant, when a creature ran across the path in front of me. My initial reaction was 'dog . . .?', then 'hare . . .?', then finally, as I was able to take in the small head, long rear legs and white patch on the tail as it fled into the distance, 'muntjac!'

That was more than twenty years ago, since when muntjacs have steadily increased in both numbers and range, and are now a common sight across much of southern and eastern Britain. Their rather endearing appearance means that many people welcome them, but like other introduced species they have no natural predators (though a fox will take one if it can), and therefore no brake on the population increasing beyond a stable, sustainable point.

Muntjac evolved in woodland, and feed on a wide range of woodland plants. Because of this, they make short work of the thick, scrubby understorey where many birds make their nest. And of all the birds threatened by the muntjac, the one in most trouble is the nightingale.

If you catch sight of a nightingale – and given this bird's skulking nature, this doesn't happen very often – prepare to be underwhelmed, for this distant relative of the robin isn't much to write home about. Some do think it striking: the early-twentieth-century ornithologist T. A. Coward called it 'a large handsome brown robin', but for most people who do manage to glimpse this elusive bird, its appearance is usually a bit of a disappointment.

Of course it wasn't the nightingale's plumage that earned it global fame, but its song, celebrated by poets from the Greeks and Romans to Keats and John Clare, in his sonnet 'The Nightingale':

> . . . I hear the Nightingale,
> That from the little blackthorn spinny steals,

To the old hazel hedge that skirts the vale,
And still unseen, sings sweet – the ploughman feels
The thrilling music, as he goes along,
And imitates and listens – while the fields
Lose all their paths in dusk, to lead him wrong
Still sings the Nightingale her sweet melodious
song.

Describing the song of a nightingale to someone who hasn't heard it is well-nigh impossible. Unlike, say, the song thrush or the blackbird, which have a limited suite of sounds and phrases, or the chaffinch or chiffchaff, which simply repeat the same phrase over and over again, the nightingale's song is a seemingly random compilation of notes that at times sounds more like a mechanical object than a bird. Yet it has a strange and compelling beauty.

Sadly, for most people, this description is the closest they are ever likely to get to actually hearing a nightingale. Since the 1970s the bird's numbers have been plummeting, and its range has also contracted, so that today nightingales can only be heard in a few isolated pockets of southern and eastern England, with fewer than 5,000 pairs remaining.

There are several likely reasons for this decline, but one of the main culprits is undoubtedly the muntjac, whose numbers have expanded hugely, and whose feeding habits are destroying the habitat which nightingales need to breed, by removing the dense scrub where they choose to build their nests. Another problem, as with so many wild creatures that are confined to the crowded south-eastern corner of Britain, is a more general loss and fragmentation of woodland habitat. This issue came to the fore when, in 2014, a council in North Kent proposed building 5,000 homes at Lodge Hill, a former military training site which now supports the largest breeding colony of nightingales in Britain: almost 100 pairs.

The ensuing row pitched two very different and competing priorities against one another: the need to build new homes to house our ever-growing human population, and the desire to preserve one of our scarcest breeding birds – along with other rare and endangered creatures such as the Duke of Burgundy butterfly. Most importantly, perhaps, Lodge Hill stood for a red line that conservationists believe should never be crossed: they argued that if we allowed development here on an SSSI (Site of Special Scientific Interest), it could happen virtually anywhere.

As a naturalist and conservationist myself, I am inclined to side with those who would fight to stop the development of this precious site; and I am also well aware that proposals to 'move the nightingales to Essex' in some kind of mitigation scheme are completely unworkable. Yet I also believe that we need more homes in the countryside, to help solve the ever-growing housing problem we are bequeathing to current and future generations. With

20,000 people on the council's waiting list, it is clear that providing homes for more than half of them would be both politically expedient and socially progressive. As the human population of these islands continues to grow, this is the kind of choice we will face more and more over the coming decades. Ultimately, I fear that the short-term needs of people are likely to triumph over the longer-term requirements of wildlife.

In the meantime, what will happen to Britain's nightingales? Whatever the final decision for those of Lodge Hill, there is now a very real danger that unless we can do something to reverse the species's rapid decline, the nightingale will disappear entirely from our shores during the next couple of decades. Some might argue that this does not really matter. Worldwide, the nightingale is still a very common bird indeed, with as many as 70 million individuals across Europe and south-west Asia; so the loss of the British population would signify very little on a global scale – at least in biological and ecological terms. But this would be to ignore the huge cultural importance of the nightingale.

Ironically, just like the dawn chorus, the nightingale's extraordinary song is simply a quirk of evolution. Over time, the male nightingales with the most varied and impressive song have attracted the most females, and thus have had a greater chance of passing on their genes to a new generation; the males of which in turn inherited the ability to sing this complex and unforgettable song.

Thanks to this quirk of evolution, we have celebrated the sound of nightingales since European culture began, and despite its scarcity, the song of no other British bird – not even the blackbird, song thrush or skylark – evokes quite such complex passions and emotions. We may allow the nightingale to slip away as a British bird, but if we do, we will have lost something that, intangible though it may be, is also a crucial part of our nation's cultural and natural heritage.

❀

MEANWHILE, ONE OF our best-known woodland mammals is also threatened, likewise from an imported species: the American grey squirrel. As most people are well aware, its presence here has devastated the population of our only native variety of squirrel, the smaller and undeniably cuter red.

The story begins in 1876, when a prosperous banker named Thomas Brocklehurst brought back a pair of grey squirrels from a business trip to North America and let them loose in the grounds of his home, Henbury Park in Cheshire. Later on in the nineteenth century, more grey squirrels were liberated in various other parts of Britain, so that by 1903, when Beatrix Potter published her famous *Tale of Squirrel Nutkin* (whose eponymous hero was a native red squirrel), a wave of greys was beginning its relentless march across the land.

By the start of the Second World War, grey squirrels could be found throughout southern Britain, with smaller numbers heading further north; by the 1960s, they had expanded their range across much of the rest of the country. This advance was mirrored by the decline of the native red squirrels, which were rapidly retreating northwards and westwards. Today the red squirrel's main strongholds are in the Scottish Highlands, the north of England and Northern Ireland, with smaller populations on offshore islands such as Anglesey, the Isle of Wight and Brownsea in Dorset, and an ecologically isolated cohort amongst the coastal pinewoods of Formby Dunes in Lancashire.

The UK population of red squirrels is thought to be about 160,000 individuals, three quarters of which are in Scotland; in stark contrast, the greys now number more than 2.5 million – more than fifteen times as many as the reds. The greys are mostly in England, with large populations living in our towns and cities, where they thrive in urban parks and by plundering bird feeders in our gardens. Grey squirrels do not simply outcompete the smaller reds; they also pass on a lethal disease, known as squirrel pox. The greys can carry this virus without being affected, but if a red squirrel should catch it, the animal suffers a slow, lingering and painful death.

Our contrasting attitudes towards the invasive grey and native red squirrels are fascinating: many people hate the greys with a deep-seated passion, and blame the incomer for the decline of the native red. Partly as a consequence of its decline, the red squirrel has become one of Britain's best-loved wild creatures, even though, as with the nightingale, most people have never even seen one.

On the other hand, many people – especially the four fifths of Britons who live in urban areas – have a sneaking admiration for the grey squirrel; perhaps because it is one of a handful of wild mammals that most city dwellers will ever encounter. Children love their antics, and some people have even constructed complex obstacle courses for them, to test their undoubted ingenuity when seeking food.

In some parts of Britain, fans of red squirrels are beginning to fight back against what they have dubbed the 'grey menace'. One project, Northern Red Squirrels, is now undertaking a concerted drive to 'control' (i.e. shoot and trap) grey squirrels, to safeguard the small and fragile populations of red squirrels still found in Cumbria and Northumberland. The group uses a combination of professional conservationists and local volunteers, and so far its efforts have been highly successful. By creating a series of cordons sanitaires around the red-squirrel areas, they have allowed the native species to recolonise its former homes including, rather appropriately, Beatrix Potter's village of Near Sawrey in the Lake District.

A similar scheme on the Welsh island of Anglesey has been even more effective. Just a decade or so ago, red squirrels were on the verge of dying out there. But thanks to a concerted campaign to eradicate the greys, backed up by local support and constant vigilance to prevent them getting back across the two land bridges to the island, reds are now flourishing.

For any conservationist this is a difficult moral and practical dilemma. We do not relish killing any wild animal, and yet if we choose not to act, the future for the red squirrel in Britain looks bleak. Within our lifetimes – and certainly by the end of the current century – the red squirrel would inevitably disappear from most of mainland Britain, and would only be found on offshore islands and perhaps in a few remote, isolated pockets of the Scottish Highlands.

The choice is simple: we can either do nothing, and allow the red squirrel's decline to continue, or we can choose to intervene. Having once been emotionally opposed to any form of culling, like many conservationists I am now coming round to a more pragmatic and interventionist approach. I now reluctantly believe that the selective killing of some alien and invasive species such as the grey squirrel is not only necessary, but a crucial weapon if we are to begin the long, slow process of restoring Britain's wildlife.

❀

THE STORY OF the red and grey squirrels reveals both the practical problems and moral dilemmas that arise when we try to save a native species; and the need to make difficult choices, which go way beyond the simple realm of science and natural history, and into cultural, moral and even political spheres. Invasive, alien species – plants and animals that do not belong in our ecosystem, but were accidentally or deliberately introduced by human agency – are often considered one of the greatest threats to our native fauna and flora, and to the biodiversity of our landscape and countryside as a whole.

There's no doubt who we should blame for these out-of-place exiles, as Christopher Lever, the acknowledged world authority on introduced animals, has pointed out in his book *The Naturalized Animals of Britain and Ireland*:

> Humans are inveterate and incorrigible meddlers, never content to leave anything as they find it but always seeking to alter and – as they see it – to improve. In no fields is this truer than in those of the animal and plant kingdoms.

Lever goes on to tell the stories of almost eighty species that have become naturalised in Britain and Ireland over the past few centuries. Some are well known, such as the rabbit, grey squirrel and Canada goose; others rather more obscure, such as the Aesculapian snake, topmouth gudgeon and midwife toad.

One important point to bear in mind is that very few 'alien species' – those that have escaped or been released into the wild in the past few hundred years – have actually managed to prosper here. Even those that have are often confined to relatively small geographical areas, where they live alongside our native species without causing too much harm. Ecologists have pointed out that Britain is not some remote oceanic island with a highly specialised fauna and flora that makes it especially vulnerable to introduced species, such as Hawaii, New Zealand or the Pacific islands.

Our wildlife is mostly very robust, partly because Britain was until relatively recently part of a much greater land mass, but also because we have had a long history of trade and interaction with other parts of the world. Introduced species (with a few notable exceptions, such as the grey squirrel) do not generally cause major problems. So perhaps we should be more relaxed about them: culling and eradicating where absolutely necessary, but otherwise choosing to live and let live where we can.

❀

IN THE MEANTIME, we do have a less urgent, but arguably more important, set of decisions to make: how should we manage our remaining woods and forests, to benefit both people and wildlife? How should we balance the competing (and sometimes mutually conflicting) needs of forestry, recreation, wildlife watching and the wild creatures themselves?

Over the years there have been some terrible environmental crimes committed by people who claimed that they had the interests of Britain's forests at heart. One infamous story from the Thatcherite boom years illustrates this perfectly. Back in the late 1970s and early 1980s, higher-rate taxpayers were offered the chance to make easy money, being granted generous tax relief to plant trees. The scheme seemed perfect: a way of making shedloads of dosh while at the same time flaunting your environmentally friendly credentials.

Unfortunately the trees were non-native conifers such as Sitka spruce, and the place they were being planted was the Flow Country, a huge expanse of blanket peat bog covering 4,000 square kilometres (1,500 square miles) of the far north of Scotland, in the counties of Caithness and Sutherland.

From a layperson's point of view, the Flow Country doesn't look all that special. Unlike the impressive mountain ranges of the Cairngorms or the western Highlands, or the river valleys of the Spey and Dee, it is flat, wet and featureless: mile after mile of boggy terrain, whose visual monotony is only broken by the patches of creamy-white cotton grass that dot this bleak and unforgiving landscape. Even the birds are few and far between: although the region is home to some of Britain's rarest breeding species, including black-throated diver, greenshank and golden plover, these do not give themselves up easily to the casual visitor. To see them at all often involves spending long hours trudging across this watery landscape, listening for their distant calls.

So it is easy to see why someone thought it would be a good idea to plant trees here; especially when the government of the day was offering generous grants and tax relief on any investment in forestry, a major incentive to higher-rate taxpayers. Celebrities such as the broadcaster Terry Wogan, snooker stars Steve Davis and Alex 'Hurricane' Higgins, and perennial pop star Cliff Richard all became involved, no doubt unaware of the disastrous environmental consequences of their investment, and encouraged by accountants and financial advisors eager to make a hefty commission.

From 1979 to 1987, thousands of acres of this unique habitat were damaged, not just by the planting of the conifers but also because the water was drained out of the land to enable the trees to grow. Finally, after almost a decade of destruction, conservationists began to appreciate what was happening, and were understandably furious. At the time, author and conservationist Sir John Lister-Kaye was chairman of RSPB Scotland. He remembers going with RSPB president Magnus Magnusson, of *Mastermind* fame, to meet the minister responsible, Sir Hector Monro. Born and raised in

Scotland, Sir Hector was the undersecretary of state in Michael Heseltine's Department of the Environment. Lister-Kaye recalls that when Magnusson played him television footage of the ploughing of the peat, which showed terrible damage to the landscape, the minister turned pale.

Within a week the tax break had been cancelled, the company responsible for the scheme then went bust, and eventually most of the investors were forced to sell their holdings. In Lister-Kaye's view, the whole scheme had been doomed from start to finish, as the trees would never have grown properly – and even if they had, the ground was so boggy the timber could never have been extracted.

The RSPB stepped in and bought a 10,000-hectare (almost 25,000 acres) area near the village of Forsinard. They then began the long, slow and laborious process of felling the trees and allowing the land to return to peat bog, a project likely to take up to a hundred years, and costing almost £3 million. Recently the RSPB has hugely extended its holding to cover many thousands of hectares, in what is now the biggest nature reserve in the UK.

This disastrous, farcical and expensive scheme can teach us valuable lessons. First, that we must always be on our guard against people with political and commercial vested interests who, when they look at a piece of land, only see the chance to make a quick profit, at whatever expense to the wildlife found there. Second, it serves as a warning that massive environmental damage can happen – and happen very rapidly – in remote places where most conservationists rarely, if ever, visit. Finally, and perhaps most importantly, it buried – hopefully for ever – the deeply held misconception that planting trees is always a good thing. As the Flow Country debacle revealed, it most definitely is not.

❀

IN MORE POPULOUS regions of Britain, woods and forests face a very different issue; but one that could prove as serious as the Flow Country forestry scheme: that of the increased demand for woodland as a place for recreation and leisure. This ranges from relatively low-impact pastimes such as wildlife watching or simply taking a walk in the woods, to potentially more problematic pursuits such as mountain biking and zip-wiring. While these are undoubtedly great fun for those who take part – and fulfil the crucial need for all of us, especially children, to take more exercise and spend more time in the outdoors – they are also potentially very damaging to individual species, including ground-nesting birds such as wood warblers and tree pipits, as well as the wider woodland environment.

In the past few decades the role of the Forestry Commission has dramatically changed. When it was founded, almost a century ago in 1919, its aim was clear and simple: to replant and expand Britain's forests after the huge depletion of woodland that had happened during the First World War, which left Britain with fewer trees than at any time in its history. The commission's success can be measured by the simple fact that it is now Britain's largest land manager, responsible for 700,000 hectares (more than 2,600 square miles) of land in England and Scotland (a separate body manages forests in Wales). But while planting and harvesting trees is still part of its responsibility, its remit has expanded hugely, to embrace scientific research, wildlife conservation and especially recreation.

Indeed, a glance at its website might lead you to conclude that recreation was the organisation's main purpose: the lead entry on the homepage lists 'visit our woods and forests . . . walking, biking' ahead of 'pests and diseases, woodfuel, woodland creation and management'. Wildlife, incidentally, doesn't get a mention.

While encouraging us to spend time in woods and forests is laudable, in some forests – especially those close to large centres of population – there are fears that this emphasis on access may be causing harm to precious (and potentially irreplaceable) wildlife habitats. In the Wyre Forest in Worcestershire, for example, local naturalists have already noticed disturbance to some species of plants and animals due, they believe, to the increased volume of activities such as uncontrolled mountain biking.

❀

THE POTENTIAL PROBLEMS that might be caused by too many people enjoying our woods and forests are at least partly offset by the obvious benefits they gain from doing so, in terms of better physical, mental and spiritual health. But the same cannot be said for another, possibly far more devastating, problem facing our woods and forests: the huge rise during the past decade or so of diseases. These don't just threaten individual trees, but have the potential to wipe out entire species, including one of our best-known and best-loved trees.

I grew up down the road from Shepperton Studios, on a 1960s housing estate on the edge of town, bordering the green belt, and backing onto what was then a quiet, almost rural lane. Amongst my earliest memories are, at four or five years old, exploring the narrow strip of trees and scrub that ran along the back of our garden. Despite its being barely a few yards wide, to us, with our limited horizons and knowledge of the world, it was an incredibly exciting place to be.

As we grew older we built dens and climbed trees, ripped off whip-like strands of poplar to use as makeshift weapons, and collected conkers from the single horse chestnut tree a few doors down the road. I can't remember who came up with the name for this, our makeshift adventure playground. It might have been one of my playmates, or it might have been passed on from previous generations of children now exploring further afield on their bikes. But for us, this place at the very epicentre of our young lives was simply 'The Forest'.

Then, just as my horizons were beginning to widen, and I was starting to discover new places to play, the Forest was no more. One morning, some time in the early 1970s, a group of men came along with their lorries and chainsaws, and in a single, devastating day of destruction, cut the trees down. The view from our kitchen window was changed for ever; in place of those tall, elegant trees there was just sky, like an ugly gap in a mouth where previously there had been a row of teeth.

The trees were, of course, English elms, and having caught Dutch elm disease – caused by a fungus carried by the elm-bark beetle – they were already doomed. Felling them was, it seemed, the only option.

All over Britain, the tragedy of this loss was made worse, because until then the English elm had been such a familiar and prominent tree in our countryside. Lines of them greeted the visitor to every rural village like a welcoming committee. Artists such as John Constable justly celebrated them; his famous painting of Salisbury Cathedral featured a massive, mature elm in the foreground, towering over the distant spire. Later, they also caught the eye of the twentieth-century artist

Rowland Hilder, whose characteristic depictions of the rural English landscape once hung in many a suburban sitting room, including our own.

So for me, as a young child whose early years had been shaped by those massive elms at the bottom of our garden, their loss was a very personal tragedy. Like the death of an old family friend, it left a pang of regret that, even after all these years, still hasn't quite faded away. And just as when you look through a photograph album, and come across a picture of someone long since departed, it stops you momentarily in your tracks, as I wander the lanes of my adopted village in Somerset I am brought up short by the unmistakable sight of an elm sapling growing in a hedgerow.

My eyes are not deceiving me: this really is an elm, sprouting vigorously above the hawthorn and blackthorn, its characteristic mid-green, rough-textured, heart-shaped leaves taking me back in an instant to my childhood. These saplings are a tribute to the tenacity of the elm. The mature trees may have all but gone, but even in death some of their roots remain alive, allowing these new trees to regenerate. Tragically, though, they are doomed to die before they reach maturity; being clones, and therefore having the same genetic make-up as their parents, they become susceptible to the disease as soon as their bark is thick enough for the fungus-bearing beetles to invade.

A decade or so before the dreaded Dutch elm disease took hold, botanical historian Geoffrey Grigson, writing in *The Englishman's Flora*, hailed the elm's versatility and beauty, and how it 'gives to English scenery much of its rich, loaded, heavy personality'. In an ironic prefiguring of the tree's eventual fate, he noted that the elm was:

> A fundamental of civilisation, of life and of death, for at last you were – and you are – buried in elm, and preferably English elm.

Thirty years after Grigson wrote those words, the English elm had all but vanished from our countryside, and the rural landscape had changed for ever. Today, these 'ghost elms', the saplings growing in the hedgerows around my village, are the only reminder of this once-familiar, and deeply loved, tree.

❁

NOW, LIKE AN unwanted sequel to a horror film, we face a new and potentially even more serious threat. Often overlooked in favour of its more familiar (and easier to identify) counterpart the oak, the tall, sprawling ash is one of the commonest and most widespread trees in Britain. It is also one of the most enduring, with some of the largest specimens being more than 400 years old – having begun their life in the reign of the first Queen Elizabeth.

The threat to the ash comes from a fungus, *Chalara fraxinea*, originally from East Asia, which was either blown across the English Channel or brought here in imported trees. Its origin is in some ways irrelevant; what does matter is that ash dieback is a serial killer of ash trees, with the same lethal effectiveness that its predecessor had for elms. It is still too early to know whether any of our ash trees might prove resistant; but by the time this decade is out, we should have a pretty clear view one way or the other.

For me, this is once again something personal. Our Somerset garden is much bigger and longer than the one where I grew up, but like my childhood home there are several mature trees at the bottom: not elm, but ash. This spring I watched anxiously as the small ash saplings first budded and then produced their characteristic sprays of lime-green leaves, the foliage filling out the shape of the tree until I could barely see the trunk. But day after day I searched in vain for the sticky black buds on the two much larger, more mature trees. Not until the middle of May did I notice any sign of life, until finally, in June, they at last began to look healthy and normal. Yet I still fear that – unless we come up with a solution to halt or slow the spread of the disease – some time over the next few years these ancient trees will wither and die, and the ash will disappear not just from my garden, my village and my county, but from all of Britain.

The likely fate of the ash sums up the way we have ignored and neglected our woodlands over years, decades and centuries. Yet as the response to the planned sell-off of our woods and forests showed, people still care deeply about these places – perhaps more than any other habitat. Restoring them to their former glory will take a lot longer than with other habitats – decades or even centuries rather than a few years. But given the central place that Britain's woodlands have in our hearts, souls and minds, we really do need to make a start.

3

Walk on the Wild Side

Mountains and Moorlands

A visitor to the British Isles usually disembarks in lowland England. He is charmed by its orderly arrangement and by its open landscapes, tamed and formed by man and mellowed by a thousand years of human history. But there is another Britain, to many of us the better half, a land of mountains and moorlands and sun and cloud . . .

W. H. Pearsall, *Mountains and Moorlands* (1950)

FAR TO THE north, in much less benign surroundings than the oak, ash and beech woodlands of southern Britain, there is a very different kind of woodland: a landscape of tall Scots pines that make up the remnants of the once-mighty Caledonian forest. Several thousand years ago, these forests would have covered much of what we know as Scotland. They are now but a fragment of what they once were, yet here in the Abernethy Forest of Strathspey, in the shadow of the snow-capped mountains of the Cairngorm Plateau, they still have the power to impress.

As soon as I step off the road and onto the path, my feet treading on a crisp carpet of fallen pine needles, I can sense the difference between this and the ancient deciduous woodlands of the south. This is no place for kicking piles of autumn leaves, or whistling the 'Teddy Bears' Picnic', though I still do so, in an unsuccessful attempt to hold down a growing sense of unease – something I always feel whenever I enter this impenetrable layer of trees that blankets the sides of the Spey Valley.

One reason for my nervousness is the silence. Whereas the woods in the south of Britain resound with birdsong, these coniferous forests are often eerily quiet. The only sounds I can hear are the occasional peep from a coal tit or goldcrest, tiny birds tucked away high in the impenetrable canopy. It is hard to escape a sense of being watched by some malevolent being – a spirit of these forbidding yet impressive forests, guarding against intruders like me.

I press on, for I have come here to try to find some of Britain's most elusive wild creatures. Yet the forest gives up its secrets grudgingly, and I will need both patience and luck if my quest is to be a success. The same is true of the mountains and moorlands that make up the rest of the Scottish Highlands: harsh, difficult places for both the wild creatures that spend their lives here and the people, like me, who come to try to see them. In this chapter I explore Britain's wildest places, and discover that even here, far away from the pressures facing the wildlife of the farmed and wooded landscapes of lowland Britain, there are still many challenges to be overcome.

❁

THESE CALEDONIAN PINE forests were formed by a unique combination of geology and climate. The ancient granite bedrock, laid down roughly 400 million years ago, is covered with a thin layer of acid, peaty soils, making it very hard for any plants to grow here. The Highlands also has one of the most unforgiving climates in the whole of Britain, so the trees that do manage to survive have to be tough. And the Scots pine is the toughest of all. With sap that acts like antifreeze, and thin, waxy needles to retain moisture, this hardy conifer is perfectly adapted to life in one of the harshest environments in the British Isles.

The Scots pine was once found much further south. Just 7,000 years ago (a blink of an eye in geological terms), during the Boreal period after the end of the last Ice Age, these tall and stately trees dominated much of southern Britain; for this was one of the few species able to cope with the dry, cool climate. But when a warmer, wetter, Atlantic-influenced climate began to dominate, the pines retreated north, to be replaced by the oak and beech woodlands we find there today.

The Scots pine found a sanctuary here in the Highlands, where its mighty forests once dominated an area of 1.5 million hectares – almost 6,000 square miles –

although there would have been significant clearings between the trees, and the total area would have waxed and waned according to fluctuations in the climate. But as demand grew for timber, for more and more land to graze sheep and cattle, and later for red-deer stalking, the forest was cut down and burned. Meanwhile, since the Bronze Age, a gradual deterioration of the climate has lowered the tree line and created blanket bog, which does not allow pine seeds to germinate and thus prevents forest regeneration. Today, as a result of these natural and man-made changes, only about 17,000 hectares (barely 60 square miles) of pine forest remains, just over 1 per cent of the original range.

Even so, the forests of the Spey Valley are mightily impressive; and I for one can easily lose my way beneath this dark canopy. This is the home of some of Britain's most localised and sought-after birds: the tiny crested tit, the mighty capercaillie, and our only endemic species, found nowhere else in the world: the Scottish crossbill.

❧

DAWN COMES EARLY to the Spey Valley; even in April, it's getting light by four in the morning, and the day's show is already under way. The waters of Loch Garten ripple in the early-morning breeze as male goldeneyes begin their courting ritual, throwing their heads back and uttering their rather mechanical call in order to impress their mates. Meanwhile, the forests alongside the shores of the loch echo to an even more bizarre sound, also to do with courtship: the mating call of the capercaillie.

The capercaillie – the name is Scots Gaelic for 'horse of the woods' – is the nearest thing we have to a wild turkey. The largest member of the grouse family anywhere in the world, a big male weighs in at over 4 kilos, and stands almost a metre high. He needs to be impressive; for his breeding strategy is based on an approach in which the winner takes it all.

As the sun begins to rise on a chilly spring morning, an unmistakable sound floats through the trees towards me; one that has been described as sounding like the recording of the opening of a bottle of champagne being played backwards. In the distance I can hear a repeated glugging, speeding up and culminating in the explosive 'pop', like a cork leaving the neck of the bottle. Peering through the trees, I see a large, dark shape moving purposefully across the needle-strewn ground, followed by a group of smaller, lighter ones. It is my first sight of a male capercaillie, performing his famous lekking display.

The word 'lek' derives from a Scandinavian word meaning 'play', and the behaviour is found in a wide and seemingly unrelated range of bird and mammal species, including several species of grouse, hummingbirds, parrots, birds-of-paradise, marine iguanas and antelopes. These very disparate groups of animals might not seem to have much in common. But in each case their food

91

source is plentiful and widely available, so the males have no need to defend a territory against their rivals. Lots of food also means that, having mated with as many females as possible, the male doesn't need to take any part in the raising of the young.

Every day, for several hours around the break of dawn, he struts up and down; tail held high and fanned out like a peacock. All the while he emits that strange chorus of popping, clicking and gurgling calls, to impress his harem of watching females. This is an all-or-nothing strategy: the dominant male gets to breed with the majority of females, who have been convinced that he is the fittest partner to ensure the continued survival of their genes through their brood of offspring.

In theory this ability to perfect the bloodline should mean that the capercaillie is thriving. And it would be, were it not for a perfect storm of factors that has pushed this mighty grouse to the brink of extinction in Britain for the second time in its history. The capercaillie first disappeared from the Caledonian pine forests some time towards the end of the eighteenth century, having been shot for sport and food, as well as suffering from the ongoing loss of its forest habitat. Half a century later, Scottish landowners brought the species back to the Highlands, releasing capercaillies from Sweden onto estates in Perthshire and later adding more birds further north, until by the end of Queen Victoria's long reign much of the Highlands had been restocked with the birds.

At the outbreak of the First World War the capercaillie could still be found across much of upland Scotland. But in the century since, the species has suffered a slow but steady decline in numbers, and today the population is thought to stand at fewer than 1,200 individuals – down from as many as 20,000 just forty years ago.

As with so many bird declines, there is no single reason for the capercaillie's catastrophic population crash. A series of wet springs has reduced breeding success, because the tiny chicks get waterlogged when following their mother through damp vegetation, and die of the resulting cold. Added to this, red-deer numbers have hugely increased since the end of the Second World War, at the same time as the proliferation of fenced commercial forestry, forcing deer to winter in old woods. Overgrazing and browsing by deer has removed the essential ground cover for the survival of capercaillie chicks.

Even if they do survive to fledging, when they finally take flight they often collide with fences erected to exclude deer from forestry plantations, which the low-flying capercaillies cannot see until it is too late. And now they face a new and unexpected threat: predation by one of Scotland's scarcest mammals, the pine marten. For years, persecution kept pine marten numbers artificially low, but now this charismatic mammal is thriving – bad news for the capercaillie. Because pine martens are rightfully protected, seemingly nothing can be done to prevent the carnage they inflict on this defenceless bird.

Conservationists are doing all they can: including removing deer fences, creating a mosaic of habitats and controlling some (though not all) predators. Yet despite their best efforts, the future for this magnificent grouse looks bleak: indeed, it is likely to go extinct here in the next decade or so. No wonder the capercaillie has recently been dubbed 'Britain's unluckiest bird'.

❀

NOT EVERY CREATURE living in these pine forests, or on the hills and moors that surround them, is in trouble. One species, the red deer – a symbol of wild Scotland for centuries – is thriving. But ironically, its success may now be causing problems for the wildlife that shares its home.

The red deer is our largest land mammal. Males weigh up to 225 kilos (more than 35 stone), almost three times as heavy as an adult human being. They sport huge, spectacular antlers, which they use each autumn to fight rival males in the annual 'rut'. As with the capercaillie's lekking display, this is a winner-takes-all contest, in which the triumphant stag wins the right to mate with his harem of females (known as hinds), while the beaten losers slink away, failures in the crucial race to reproduce. But there is far more to this animal than simply its biology and behaviour. Along with a select few species, such as the golden eagle, the red deer has become a potent emblem of its Highland home.

Deer have always been considered majestic animals – as well as being exploited in a practical way for their food and skins – but their status rose rapidly in the mid-nineteenth century. This was largely down to a single, iconic image: the oil painting *The Monarch of the Glen*, completed in 1851 by an English artist, Sir Edwin Landseer, which celebrated the new fashion for deer stalking endorsed by Queen Victoria and Prince Albert. The painting, which is on permanent display at the National Museum of Scotland in Edinburgh, depicts a lone red deer stag, standing proudly against a glowering sky with distant mountains in the background, antlers held aloft in triumph.

Nowadays this undeniably striking and powerful picture has been so widely reproduced, copied and parodied that it has become a visual cliché – indeed, one journalist called it 'the ultimate biscuit-tin image of Scotland'. But at the time of its first public appearance the work was widely celebrated, helping to cement the fame of the Highlands for generations afterwards, and propelling the red deer towards the top of the list of Britain's favourite wild animals.

This may explain our reluctance to face the facts: that there are now simply far too many deer in the Scottish Highlands: roughly 400,000 red deer and up to 350,000 of our other native, the smaller roe deer. Both these species are destroying habitats and causing problems to many of the wild creatures that live there. Their continual browsing thins out the woodland understorey, while the pressure from hundreds of hooves trampling across hills and mountainsides causes soil erosion and can lead to flooding. Meanwhile, the erection of deer fences to prevent the animals entering a particular area has, as we've seen, contributed to the decline of the capercaillie.

There is, however, another issue here: both red and roe deer are not simply wild animals, but also an important economic resource. Deer stalking has always been a popular pastime, but in recent years it has developed into a major industry, charging wealthy clients up to £500 for each stag they shoot, and generating an estimated £70 million a year for the Scottish economy. This profit must, however, be at least partly offset by the damage caused by browsing deer – Forestry Commission Scotland spend a minimum of £10 million a year on controlling deer to protect their growing trees, while farmers, too, have to cope with deer on their land. Deer are also a major cause of road-traffic accidents, with thousands of collisions costing an estimated £9.4 million in Scotland alone, and causing hundreds of injuries and the occasional tragic death of a motorist.

The reason for the rise of the deer population is quite simple: there are no big predators to keep the numbers in check. Until the medieval period, the forests and hills of the Highlands were home to packs of wolves, which held deer numbers down by regular predation. Earlier still, brown bears and Eurasian lynxes roamed this landscape until they, like the wolf, were persecuted into extinction. In the absence of these predators, numbers of both red and roe deer have risen inexorably, which now presents us with problems for farmers, foresters, motorists and of course other wildlife.

The biggest irony of all is that there are now two mutually opposed sides in the debate of what to do about the red-deer problem: one favouring culling, the other against it. But whereas you might expect those against the killing of our best-loved native mammals to be the conservationists, the opposite is the case. The conservationists are calling for the deer to be culled, to bring numbers back into balance with the available habitat, while the shooters – concerned that any reduction in numbers will lead to a loss of income from deer stalking – are standing firmly against any cull. Such is the topsy-turvy world of modern conservation.

But culling, although effective in the short term, is by no means the best solution. In the longer term we need to bring back those lost apex predators, to restore the balance at the top of the food chain. Releasing packs of wolves or brown bears into the relatively populous Scottish Highlands might not be politically or socially acceptable (though it would be highly effective at keeping deer numbers down), but the reintroduction of a smaller predator, the lynx, could work rather well.

Despite its relatively small size – males reach just over a metre long and weigh about 30 kilos (66 pounds, or about the same as an eleven-year-old child) – the lynx is a formidable predator. It moves like a ghost, stalking its potential victim slowly and very patiently until it gets close enough to pounce. The deer is completely unaware that it is being hunted until it feels the lynx's claws on its back, followed by the animal's teeth sinking into its neck.

Lynx disappeared from Britain well over 1,000 years ago, and by the end of the nineteenth century had been driven close to extinction in the rest of mainland Europe too. But since then, this secretive beast has made a comeback, and can now be found in the wilder regions of the Pyrenees, parts of Scandinavia and the Balkans. The species has also been successfully reintroduced into several European countries, including France, Germany and Italy, where it now thrives in small but growing numbers. In theory, this animal could be reintroduced to Britain: indeed, a new organisation, the Lynx UK Trust, has already applied for a licence to begin a controlled reintroduction scheme in forests in the remote western Highlands.

In practice, though, the scheme faces considerable barriers, not least the vocal opposition of a small number of influential landowners and sheep farmers. Scottish landowners, with a few notable exceptions, do not have a good track record when it comes to welcoming species-reintroduction schemes. This is partly because of the potential for collateral damage to farm livestock or red grouse, but mainly, perhaps, because of a long-held antipathy towards wildlife-and-conservation groups in the Scottish Highlands, built up over many decades.

Just imagine for a moment the benefits of the return of Europe's third-largest predator to Scotland's forests, hills and mountains. Not just the reduction in deer numbers, and the rebalancing of the natural ecosystem by the reappearance of an animal at the top of the food chain; but also the economic advantages brought by the many thousands of people who would flock to the Highlands with the hope of catching a glimpse of this magnificent animal.

❦

IT IS IRONIC that at a point when we are seriously considering bringing back one large feline predator into the Scottish Highlands, we stand on the very brink of losing another. This time, that loss would not just be a local calamity, but also a global one. For *Felis silvestris grampia*, the 'Highland tiger' – better known as the Scottish wildcat – is a race unique to these islands, having been separated from its cousins across Europe and Asia for more than 100,000 years.

In the absence of bears, wolves and lynxes, the Scottish wildcat is Britain's largest native predator. It is also by far the rarest large mammal in Britain: recent estimates of its numbers have ranged from four hundred individuals to fewer than fifty. Unless we can do something to save the Scottish wildcat – and very soon – it is doomed to extinction within the next decade, possibly even earlier.

The story of the demise of the wildcat is in part a familiar one – but with an unexpected modern twist. Once found all over Britain, the wildcat disappeared from England and Wales during the nineteenth century, being gradually driven northwards into its current home in the remote glens, forests and mountains of the Scottish Highlands, where a handful still survive.

Its decline was, at least at first, the result of the usual suspects: the loss of extensive woodland habitat, along with centuries of persecution. But in these more enlightened times, we might surely expect the wildcat to be making a comeback. And indeed it would be, were it not for the presence of a close relative in its Highland home: about 100,000 once-domesticated cats, which have now gone feral – just part of an army of well over 1 million cats on the loose in Britain as a whole.

These animals are smaller and weaker than the wildcats, and so when a male wildcat encounters a female feral one, the inevitable coupling occurs. From then on the female feral cat's offspring – and their offspring, on and on down the generations – carry the genes of the once-domesticated tabby, as well as those of the true wildcat. Over time, this dilutes the genetic make-up of most wild animals, so that today it is possible that only a tiny handful of pure-bred Scottish wildcats remain – perhaps none at all.

One drastic but effective way to stem the decline would be to instigate the culling of any feral cats living within the wildcat's range. But as well as its being logistically very difficult, we can easily imagine the outcry from Britain's cat-lovers should such a mass cull go ahead. Few politicians – either at Holyrood or Westminster – would consider such a potentially career-ending decision.

In the meantime Scottish Natural Heritage (SNH), the government agency responsible for conserving all Scotland's wildlife, is working with the owners of large estates and cat-welfare charities to control and neuter feral cats, while trying to collate sightings of any potential pure-bred animals.

This scheme – costing more than £2 million – has come in for some criticism. Once again, as seems to happen in Scotland more than any other part of the UK, the battle lines have been drawn up between two groups of people who one might imagine would be on the same side, but who appear to have taken implacably opposed standpoints.

In one corner, SNH champions what it calls its 'pragmatic' approach; in the other, a small and outspoken band of conservationists believe that far more drastic action needs to be taken. They have attracted support from some commentators in the media, one of whom has described the response of SNH as 'a mixture of complacency [and] incompetence', and of 'being actively complicit in the extinction of this wild and beautiful Scottish beast'.

What the other group proposes instead is a three-stage process. First, to catch as many 'wildcats' as they can and test them genetically to find out which – if any – are pure-bred. Then, take those that are close to 100 per cent pure wildcats to 'ark sites' on the Ardnamurchan Peninsula in the west of Scotland. Here, they can potentially be isolated from the risk of interbreeding with feral cats. Finally, begin a properly funded programme of neutering feral cats elsewhere in the Highlands, where pure-bred wildcats might either still survive or could eventually be reintroduced.

Deciding who is right in this bitter and complex dispute is tricky, given the clash of vested interests and opinions involved. The latter scheme may sound sensible, but in practice it is fraught with problems; not least the fact that those involved have cut their ties with the conservation establishment, and are not sharing their data or allowing it to be peer-reviewed. And despite what is often said in the media, the SNH is carrying out trapping and testing of DNA, neutering feral cats and monitoring suitable habitat.

Like the vast majority of people in Britain, and even many of those living in the Highlands, I have never seen a Scottish wildcat – and I suspect that I never shall. This raises a crucial question, a question similar to that raised by the demise of the nightingale and red squirrel: Does it matter if this animal ultimately disappears from Britain? In this case, as well as the cultural arguments for saving the wildcat, there is an ecological one too: if it goes, we shall have lost this distinctive race for ever. We should – and indeed do – care about any wild animal faced with extinction, for its loss is a loss for us all. In the words of the seventeenth-century poet and priest John Donne:

> Any man's death diminishes me,
> Because I am involved in mankind;
> And therefore never send to know for whom the
> bell tolls;
> It tolls for thee.

For the Scottish wildcat, the bell is already tolling, and it may soon fall silent. That truly would diminish us all.

❁

AS WE CONTEMPLATE the bleak future of the Scottish wildcat, we can at least take comfort in the notion that the forests and hills where the last few wildcats roam are some of our few truly unspoilt places, as close to wild landscape as we can get in this crowded island of more than 60 million people. And how much wilder is the place that towers above them: the high tops of the Cairngorm Plateau, the coldest, harshest and most remote part of the British Isles. Surely these majestic mountains remain untouched by human hand, providing an undisturbed haven for their specialised, and very special, wildlife.

Yet over centuries, right up to the present day, the Cairngorm Mountains, along with the valleys, hills and forests below them, have been the subject of more conflicts, controversies and misconceptions than almost any other region of Britain. They have been fought over by farmers and foresters, deer hunters and grouse shooters, salmon fishermen and skiers, mountain climbers and birdwatchers. This shows that nowhere in Britain, however remote and inaccessible, is free from dispute over the way it should be used and managed for people and wildlife. Despite appearances, this place is not by any true definition a wilderness: the land here is owned and managed just like any other part of Britain, and just like anywhere else, humans and wildlife compete for the same limited space.

❀

As I walk away from the Ptarmigan Restaurant on this chilly spring day, three quarters of the way towards the summit of Cairn Gorm, I enter a very different world from the wooded valleys just 1,000 feet or so below. An impressive vista opens up before me: crags and peaks, light and shade, and above all snow – great piles of the stuff, as if a movie director has decided that he must have a White Christmas scene in the middle of May.

I trudge forward, heading south towards the peak of Scotland's second-highest mountain, Ben Macdui.

Queen Victoria described reaching the top of Ben Macdui as having 'a sublime and solemn effect, so wild, so solitary . . .' Working out the distance ahead of me, and taking into account my slow pace as I sink up to my knees in the powdery snow at every step, I somehow don't think I'll be emulating her climb today.

After a good fifteen minutes' walking through the snow, skirting the side of Cairn Gorm, I have yet to see a single living creature, apart from the odd passing skier clad in luminous orange and red. Unused to this, I am beginning to hallucinate: Is that rock a mountain hare? Could that dark shadow on that distant crag be a golden eagle?

Superficially, there would appear to be very good reasons for this lack of wildlife. What creature in its right mind would choose to live here, where the climate is so bleak, food and shelter so hard to find, and life so harsh? But there is a flip side to this: any creature tough enough to survive will have a clear run, with few competitors or predators to make life difficult.

Then a sound drifts on the stiff breeze towards me: a rapid series of loud clicks, followed by a rasping croak. Two plump birds appear from beneath the shelter of a tall, granite rock. They are about the size and shape of bantam chickens, lichen-grey on the head, breast and back, and white below, reflecting the snow: a pair of ptarmigans.

The ptarmigan is unique amongst British birds in having three distinct plumages during the course of a single year. In the summer, they are mottled in various shades of buff and brown, to match the new heather; in autumn they turn lichen-grey, enabling them to blend in with the granite rocks that strew this bleak landscape like discarded litter; and as the winter snows arrive they turn white. By changing shade as the seasons themselves change, the ptarmigan can hide from predators, and so survive in this constantly shifting landscape.

I stand still in the lee of a rock as the birds move hesitantly forward, tentatively plucking sprigs of heather and lichen from the few snow-free patches. Although feeding, they are constantly on the lookout for danger: their main predator is the golden eagle, which soars over vast areas of this harsh landscape searching for ptarmigan below.

Out of the corner of my eye, I see a small, sleek shape streaking across the valley below me. The ptarmigan see it too, and cower momentarily, their plumage blending perfectly in with the heather and moss amongst which they are hiding. For them it is a false alarm, but for me an exciting moment: a merlin, Britain's smallest bird of prey. This tiny, gunmetal-grey falcon, barely the size of a mistle thrush, lives up to his name by being a true magician, appearing out of nowhere to chase meadow pipits and skylarks, which it hunts down with ruthless efficiency.

When I look back, the ptarmigan have disappeared.

❀

APART FROM THE ptarmigan and the odd golden eagle, only three other creatures spend the whole of the year here. Just like the former, two of them turn white to help camouflage themselves in the predominantly snow-covered landscape. One, the stoat, is a predator; the other, the mountain hare, its intended prey. If the ptarmigan is our toughest bird, these are rivals for the title of Britain's hardiest mammal.

On my second visit to Cairn Gorm, this time in the middle of winter, there is one more creature for me to see. I find a small flock around the Ptarmigan Restaurant itself, living off crumbs dropped by passing visitors. As I approach they take to the air in a rush of wings, revealing flashes of white like falling snowflakes against the darkening grey background.

These are snow buntings, the archetypal Arctic bird; alternative Scots names include 'snow flake', 'snaw foul' and 'snow fleck'. The snow bunting gives the ptarmigan a close run for its money as not just Britain's toughest bird, but also one of the hardiest in the world. It is one of only three species – along with the kittiwake and fulmar – that has been recorded at the North Pole itself.

Many birds from this wintering flock in the Cairngorms will leave by the spring, heading north to breed in Iceland or Scandinavia. But a handful will stay on here to nest in the rocky, snow-covered corries of the plateau, singing their rhythmic and tuneful song from the tops of huge granite boulders.

You might imagine that the snow buntings – and the other creatures tough enough to live here – would be able to go about their lives largely undisturbed on this high, wild plateau; unaffected by the massive changes happening thousands of feet below in the crowded, contested lowlands. Yet in fact they are amongst the most threatened of all our wild creatures: their habitat is the only one in Britain predicted to disappear during the current century.

The reason is not the usual story we have seen in the South – pesticides, pollution, population growth, unbridled development and habitat fragmentation – for the Cairngorms are mostly isolated from such problems. But they cannot escape from the threat of global climate change. A rise in temperature over the next hundred years of just one or two degrees (and many reliable scientific predictions suggest a much greater rise than this) would irrevocably change the delicate ecosystem here in two key ways.

Over time, rising temperatures would allow lowland vegetation such as heather to move up the mountainside, bringing with it creatures that would begin to compete with the upland specialists, and plants that would completely change the habitat here. In the longer term, climate change would also alter the nature of the landscape itself by disrupting the cycle of snow, the freezing and thawing of which these species depend on for their livelihood.

Ironically, by adapting so well to life in this harsh and highly specialised environment, creatures such as the ptarmigan, mountain hare and snow bunting have boxed themselves into an ecological dead end. If and when change does occur, they will simply have nowhere else to go.

Watching the sparrow-sized snow buntings pecking at tiny morsels of food in the snow, as I lose all feeling in my hands and feet, it is hard to believe that this unique habitat could disappear within my lifetime. Yet if global warming does, as predicted, continue, then that is exactly what will happen – and there is nothing we can do to prevent it.

❊

LOWER DOWN, THE hills of much of Scotland and the upland areas of northern England are covered with a blanket of heather. Also known as ling, heath and, more poetically, 'mountain mist', heather is the classic upland plant of late summer. Great swathes of it turn vast areas of moorland purple, and become – in the words of botanical historian Geoffrey Grigson – 'a favourite symbol of bad artists and makers of the picture postcard'.

Heather is one of those plants on which our ancestors depended for a whole range of products. It was used to make brooms or besoms (hence the Somerset folk name 'bissom'), rope, baskets and even beer. Heather was also used as thatch for cottage roofs, and when dried, burned as fuel.

Aside from the traditional uses of heather exploited by our ancestors, it's hard to imagine why anyone would be interested in this bleak and unforgiving landscape. And yet they certainly are. A glance at the website of the exclusive property agent Savills reveals a number of Scottish estates for sale at eye-watering prices.

Come here on 12 August, and you'll soon discover why. For that day, the so-called 'Glorious Twelfth', is the start of the grouse-shooting season. And just like deer stalking, grouse shooting is an important part of the Scottish rural economy.

The red grouse depends on heather moorland more than any other bird. Its very colours seem to mimic its surroundings: a deep, rich reddish-brown, mottled and flecked with greys and blacks, and set off with the male's bright crimson wattle above the eye, giving him a permanently surprised expression.

This camouflage allows grouse to stay hidden until you are almost on top of them, when they take to the air in a noisy flurry of wings accompanied by a wonderfully human-sounding 'go-back, go-back, go-back' as they whirr away from you at great speed.

Red grouse are tough little birds too: not quite as hardy as their cousin the ptarmigan, but still able to survive on these bleak moors throughout the year. They are extremely sedentary – few ever venture more than a mile or two from where they were hatched – and feed mostly on the tender shoots and leaves of young heather, though they will also take insects such as crane flies in late summer and early autumn.

Proponents of grouse shooting like to claim that it is a long and ancient tradition, dating back centuries. But although the first unfortunate bird to fall to a gun died in the middle of the seventeenth century, the practice of 'driven grouse shooting', using beaters to flush the birds into the fire of the guns, is a late-Victorian phenomenon, barely more than a century old.

Shooting grouse may be a cripplingly expensive pastime, but to own a grouse moor you need to be pretty wealthy too. The owner has to maintain the habitat outside the shooting season by burning areas to allow new heather to grow, keep an army of gamekeepers and beaters to push the birds towards the guns, and supply all the visiting shooters with the finest refreshments and accommodation.

So anything that threatens to reduce the number of grouse available for shooting is regarded as the enemy. And that's why one native British bird – the hen harrier – is, despite being a legally protected species, regularly being shot, trapped and killed to protect the economic interests of a tiny minority of people: the owners of grouse moors. Hen harriers are just as much part of our national heritage as any precious work of art; and yet their senseless killing goes on with barely a whisper of protest from politicians or the press.

It's safe to say that typical owners of grouse moors are unlikely to be the hen harrier's biggest fans. They hate all raptors, but save a special vitriol for the hen harrier, which does take young grouse, along with its more usual prey of mice, voles and meadow pipits. But their response is entirely disproportionate: the deliberate – and let's not forget illegal – targeting and killing of hen harriers, resulting in their current absence from large swathes of northern Britain.

Like all harriers, the hen harrier is slender and long-winged, with a floating, buoyant flight that instantly marks it out as something different from the stockier and more pedestrian buzzards that share its upland habitat. Females and immatures – known as 'ringtails' because of the dark bands across the upper tail – are mainly brown, with a white rump that lights up like a beacon when they fly into roost at the end of a short winter's day. But it is the males that are truly breathtaking: a pale blueish-grey, with a narrow white rump, piercing yellow eyes, and wings that look as if the tips have been dipped in black ink.

Hundreds of hen harriers are illegally shot each year. As a result the UK population, which should be about 2,500 pairs, is less than one third of that number – and virtually confined to those parts of Scotland where grouse shooting is not a major industry, such as Orkney and the Western Isles. In England, things are even worse: in 2013, for the first time in recorded history, not a single pair of hen harriers successfully bred south of the Scottish border, even though there is enough moorland habitat to support at least 300 breeding pairs.

More than sixty years ago, in June 1954, a crucial piece of legislation became law. The Protection of Birds Act provided legal safeguards to the vast majority of Britain's birds, meaning that apart from a few pest species such as rooks and crows, all were protected against being killed, or their nests and eggs being destroyed. Yet today, in the twenty-first century, there are even fewer hen harriers than there were then. This is despite the fact that most other birds of prey have seen huge population rises in the intervening decades, thanks partly to a reduction in persecution but also to the banning of lethal pesticides such as DDT.

So the case against the shooters of hen harriers is clear-cut: they are wilfully and deliberately breaking the law. Were they doing so in more populated areas of southern Britain, where they might be seen, they would be caught in the act more often than they are. But because they are doing their killing on vast private estates, inaccessible to both the public and the police, and because the landowners who employ them are rich and influential, they are getting away with it – time and time again. If they are found guilty, the punishments are derisory; fines of a few hundred pounds, along with suspended prison sentences, which mean that even if they are caught and prosecuted, the killing of hen harriers is still economically worthwhile.

But perhaps things are starting to change. First, the law in Scotland is now able to prosecute landowners under the term 'vicarious liability', so that they are responsible for any wrongdoing by their employees, even if they claim they were unaware of it. Meanwhile, sickened by the constant killing of these birds, and frustrated by the lack of action from both the legal authorities and conservation organisations, former RSPB director of conservation Mark Avery has organised a petition against the illegal killing of hen harriers.

The petition calls for the banning of driven grouse shooting, and has been accompanied by protests on the moors themselves, and a consumer boycott of shops and restaurants that sell grouse; a boycott that very swiftly led Marks & Spencer to stop stocking the product. Whether the bigger campaign for a total ban will ultimately succeed is perhaps unlikely, given the powerful vested interests ranged against it; but anything that draws attention to illegal raptor persecution must be a good thing.

❀

WHAT WOULD HAPPEN to this land if shooting did end is uncertain. Although if well managed, Britain's uplands could support a range of wildlife, it is more likely that most moors will revert to farmland. They'll probably end up being covered with sheep: in the memorable term coined by environmental writer George Monbiot, 'sheep-wrecked'. Ironically, this could mean the death knell for the red grouse, showing once again that when we try to solve one environmental problem we sometimes inadvertently create others.

The alternative, however, is simply not acceptable: that we continue to allow the intensive farming of a wild bird, wiping out every potential predator or competitor simply to satisfy the warped tastes of a few, and make a profit for even fewer.

There is one possible solution: recent studies have shown that when supplementary food is provided for hen harriers on grouse moors, in the form of day-old chicks and white rats, then predation levels fall, allowing both harriers and grouse to coexist. Like all interventions this costs money; but given that the owners of grouse moors are eligible for the single-farm payment (which for a large shooting estate can mean an annual subsidy from the taxpayer of tens of thousands of pounds), they could reasonably be expected at least to contribute to the costs.

However, prominent environmentalists such as Richard Mabey have denounced this as simply protecting the grouse-shooting industry and failing to tackle the problem at the heart of the issue – the fact that hen harriers are being shot, and that this is against the law. He has a point.

The fate of both these unique and wonderful birds – the hen harrier and the red grouse – is now finely balanced. Ultimately the future of Britain's uplands may depend on finding a workable solution to this apparently intractable problem.

❀

THE FUTURE OF Britain's uplands is – as with farmland and woodland – dependent on many complex and interwoven factors. These range from the purely political, such as who owns the land and what they are allowed to do on it, to the biological and ecological, such as how we best manage these diverse landscapes to benefit the wild creatures tough enough to live there.

It may seem to be a daunting task – and it is – but we can learn a lesson from another habitat that, not much more than fifty years ago, was one of the most damaged and degraded of all, but is now mostly thriving: that of Britain's rivers.

4

Messing About with Our Rivers

Rivers and Streams

No man ever steps into the same river twice – for it is not
the same river, and he is not the same man.

Heraclitus of Ephesus (*c*.500 BC)

ON A WARM afternoon in the middle of an unexpectedly
fine English summer, there are few more relaxing places
to be than sitting by a chalk stream in the heart of Dorset.
From a rickety wooden bridge I gaze downstream, and
in a moment find myself completely mesmerised by the
water's flow.

It is this constantly flowing, always dynamic nature
of rivers that creates the most changeable and exciting
of all Britain's wildlife habitats. This ongoing tension
between permanence and transience makes them crucially
important for wildlife.

Our rivers and streams provide a vital place for birds,
mammals, fish, reptiles and amphibians to feed and
drink, and opportunities for them to breed and nest.
Most importantly they are natural corridors, allowing
wild creatures to move from one place to another with

ease, both up- and downstream. From eels to otters, mallards to mayflies, and dippers to dragonflies, river creatures are a crucial part of the jigsaw of Britain's natural heritage.

But rivers can also be a really tough place for wildlife to live. Their constantly changing nature means they are as challenging as they are rewarding, and river creatures need to adapt to cope with the changes in water flow and level that can occur very rapidly indeed. Becoming too specialised can also prove problematic, however. Paradoxically, the better suited a creature becomes to living in this unique habitat, the more vulnerable it is to change. If something does go wrong, it has nowhere else to go.

During the late 1970s and early 1980s, many of Britain's rivers were almost destroyed. Ironically, the intention was the very opposite: the plan was to 'improve' them in a quest to make them flow more easily – straightening the banks, dredging the beds and clearing vegetation. But the result was disastrous for our river wildlife: by simplifying the nature of these complex watercourses, these changes destroyed the myriad microhabitats required for life to thrive here.

Like all wild creatures, those that live in rivers and streams need complexity: shallow pools where they can lay their eggs; faster-flowing stretches where they feed; and nooks and crannies where they can hide away from predators. The homogenising of the river habitat destroyed this complexity, and our rivers and their wildlife suffered as a result. Ironically, the changes didn't even fulfil their aim of reducing the risk of flooding: because the waters were allowed to run faster, the flood risk was actually increased further downstream.

During the past few decades the situation has been completely reversed. Rivers and streams that were, biologically speaking, dead, are now packed with wildlife. They have been restored to their former glory by the introduction of legislation to prevent the dumping of chemicals and sewage, landscaping to repair the damage done by the attempts at 'improvement', and measures to create a mosaic of habitats where wildlife can thrive. And as often happens when changes are made to help nature, we have benefited too; for the more complex and slower-flowing a river is, the less likely it is to flood.

❀

AT FIRST GLANCE, when you gaze at a river there may seem to be very little going on. But even on this hot summer's afternoon I can see stick-like damselflies rising from the surface, hovering on their sylph-like wings, as they look out for larger, predatory dragonflies like the four-spotted chaser perching on a reed stem nearby. The dragonfly's wings are held out at a 90-degree angle from its body, so that when backlit by the sun, its silhouette resembles a First World War biplane.

I move closer, and change my angle of view so that I can see the insect better. No matter how often I look at a dragonfly, I never fail to be amazed by its sheer beauty, combined with a clinical efficiency of purpose. Few other insects, indeed few other living creatures, combine form and function quite so perfectly.

Its streamlined, cigar-shaped body is a little shorter than my thumb, and about half as broad. It is the colour of burnished bronze, etched with ultra-thin yellow lines, as if decorated with gold leaf. The four wings are so delicate they look as if they could snap off at any moment, and yet so strong they can propel the dragonfly at speeds of 30 miles an hour as it patrols up and down the banks of the stream, searching for the smaller insects on which it feeds.

The chaser seems settled, so I risk a closer approach. From a couple of metres away I can see every detail of this stunning creature, including the eight dark spots – two on each wing – that make this one of the easiest dragonflies to identify. At such close range I can also see the delicate criss-cross membrane of the wing, a complex latticework of individual tiny panels welded together to create the whole structure. Suddenly, with a rapid flick of its wings, the dragonfly is airborne. It hovers for a brief moment right in front of me and then, with an agility that would put a helicopter to shame, it turns and is away, disappearing along the stream.

For a few minutes, I have been entirely transported into the world of this beautiful and enthralling insect; so much so that I have almost forgotten where I am. Brought back to reality, I become aware that for the past minute or so I have been hearing a distant and persistent call – a series of high-pitched notes battering into my brain. I hear it again – this time closer – and then I see the maker of the sound, as a flash of impossibly bright blue and deepest orange shoots past me and heads away downstream: a kingfisher.

I lift my binoculars just in time to be dazzled by a tiny, jewel-like bird as it disappears around the bend, its call lingering in the air like the azure flash it leaves behind on my retina. Meanwhile, below me, a pair of white swans drifts along, floating effortlessly on the surface of the water and occasionally dipping their bills beneath to grab a beakful of waterweed.

The contrast between the frantic movement of the kingfisher and the studied nonchalance of the swans sums up, once again, the paradox of rivers: the constant tension between stasis and movement that creates and sustains all life here. As the Greek philosopher Heraclitus also wrote, 'Everything flows, nothing stands still'.

❁

THERE ARE WELL over 1,000 different rivers and streams in Britain, and few of us live more than a mile or so from one. Rivers are the arteries and veins of our landscape, carrying its lifeblood – fresh, clean water – throughout the country. Each one flows inexorably downwards from its source in the hills and mountains, wending a leisurely path through towns and villages, fields and woods, countryside and cities, before finally reaching its destination: the open sea.

Rivers criss-cross the country in a network that was here long before roads and railways ever appeared, and which will remain long after they have gone. Rivers also run through the heart of urban Britain: virtually every major British city, from London to Liverpool, Cardiff to Norwich and Aberdeen to Plymouth, is built on a river.

Rivers themselves are also very susceptible to change. The crystal-clear waters of this Dorset stream may look fresh and pure, but this could alter in an instant. Chemical spills, run-off from agricultural pesticides, and human sewage are just three of the threats that could destroy all life here. Even if such a man-made disaster does not arise, river wildlife must still cope with the shifts in water flow brought about by drought and flood, suffer disturbance from people, and deal with accidental or deliberate changes to the riverbanks themselves.

The story of Britain's rivers and their precious wildlife is one that encompasses all these problems and more. It is a story that starts with decline and ruin, when we almost lost our river wildlife for ever. But it is also a story of hope and renewal, in which the tide did finally turn, and our rivers and streams came back to life once again.

Compared with the plight of our farmland, woodland and upland wildlife, rivers represent a (perhaps unexpected) success; hope in an otherwise grim world. But as the recent history of our rivers reveals, we can never afford to be complacent, for even though wild creatures have made a comeback during the past few decades, they could easily be lost once again.

We begin in the years following the Second World War, on one of the most famous rivers in Britain, about as different from this peaceful Dorset stream as can be imagined: the Tyne.

❀

SATURDAY NIGHT IN Newcastle city centre might seem an odd place, and an even odder time, to look for wildlife on Britain's rivers. Mind you, life here can be pretty wild: the girls queuing outside the nightclubs, wearing impossibly short skirts and skimpy tops despite the chilly air; the lads clad in their black-and-white striped Newcastle United shirts, necking cans of lager as if their life depended on it; and the booming sound of music echoing from every doorway, provided by multiple DJs for the entertainment of the crowds.

Newcastle has changed beyond recognition in the past few decades. Mining, shipbuilding and other heavy industries, which sustained this great city for more than two centuries from the start of the Industrial Revolution into the 1970s, closed down within just a few years. The city and its people could have fallen into terminal decline, but instead it has been reborn as a centre for new technology and culture. What anyone who remembers Newcastle from the 1950s era of Jackie Milburn and brown ale would think of the city today – with its boutiques and galleries, high-tech industries and highly paid foreign footballers – is hard to imagine.

Industry and nature are uneasy bedfellows at the best of times, but the heavy industry that sustained Tyneside and its people for so many years was an unmitigated disaster for the city's wildlife. During the post-war boom, as heavy industry deposited its waste products straight into its waters, the River Tyne became a byword for pollution – the dirtiest river in Britain. In the late 1950s even the local MP described the Tyne as 'deplorable, intolerable and indecent', and local wags joked that you didn't need to be Jesus Christ to be able to walk from one side to the other without getting your feet wet.

Today, just over half a century later, Tyneside's wildlife is unrecognisably different. Upstream, kingfishers and salmon have returned, while downstream, around the city centre itself, there are completely new arrivals. As

I walk along the towpath, and pass beneath the famous railway bridge, I hear a soft, familiar cry above my head: 'kitt-i-waaake . . . kitt-i-waaake . . .' This is the sound of the most marine and arguably the prettiest of all our gulls, the kittiwake, calling out its name.

In the gathering gloom I can just make out the gleaming, soap-powder whiteness of their plumage, as a dozen or more birds perch on their nests 50 feet above my head. Back in the days when the river was a powerhouse of industry, the nearest place you could see kittiwakes was 10 miles downstream, at Tynemouth, where the river deposits its waters into the North Sea.

These elegant seabirds first arrived in the city centre a couple of decades ago, when a pioneering pair nested on the window ledges of the derelict Baltic Flour Mill, just across the river in Gateshead. When the mill was later converted into a contemporary art gallery, the birds simply moved onto the metal girders of the railway bridge, where they have been in residence ever since. They thrive here because they are safe: safer than on the cliffs around our coasts, where marauding herring gulls and great black-backed gulls seize the chicks and their eggs. It's a fine example of a wild creature's ability to adapt to change, and prosper as a result.

Not that the local residents have always appreciated this newcomer in their midst. They have even been known to complain about the noise of the kittiwakes – which is a bit rich given the nightclub cacophony that still rings in my ears as I wander upstream. At least they notice the birds; but they are less likely to be aware of the creature I am searching for, as its nocturnal habits mean that it is rarely seen. Only the angler waiting patiently for a bite as he settles in for the night on the north bank of the Tyne is likely to catch a glimpse of this elusive animal.

We nod companionably to each other as I walk past; both wishing the music could be turned down a little. As recently as thirty years ago this old boy would have had a long time to wait before he caught any fish. In those days the Tyne was still the most polluted river in Britain – a remarkable if unwanted accolade, given the dire state of the Tees, Trent and Thames.

During a century and more of industrial progress, millions of gallons of sewage and chemicals had poured into the Tyne, turning it from a once-clear, sparkling river into a muddy brown soup, lethal to any wild creature that dared to venture into its waters. Finding a fish – any fish – here in the 1950s would have been quite a challenge. Yet today the Tyne, along with all the other major British rivers, has been transformed, partly through the passing and enforcement of strong legislation to halt the pollution, and partly because – here at least – the heavy industries that once sat along the river's banks have long since disappeared.

One creature disappeared from the Tyne during that dreadful post-war period of pollution and persecution;

and only returned here, and to many other rivers up and down the country, a decade or so ago. It is this creature I hope to encounter tonight.

❀

THE SOUNDS OF the nightclubs finally begin to fade, as I leave the lights of the city behind me. Fortunately there is a full moon, so I can see the river; the tide is rising, and swirling waters begin to engulf the exposed shores. In the distance, a lone redshank hurriedly probes for food in the rapidly disappearing mud. Seeing me, it launches itself upstream, its echoing alarm call fading into the darkness.

I choose a suitable spot and settle myself down on the riverbank. I could be in for a long wait – the animal I'm looking for may be here, but that doesn't mean it will be easy to see. Half an hour passes; then an hour; and my feet begin to go numb with the cold. And then, just as I am thinking about heading back to my city-centre hotel, I see it: a thin trail of bubbles along the glassy surface of the river, heading my way. I gingerly lift my binoculars, hardly able to contain my excitement; and as I do so something emerges from the water.

A rounded head, complete with snub nose and whiskers from which drops of water fall back into the river, is swiftly followed by a long, sleek body dipping just above the water's surface, and the hint of a tail behind. It moves quickly, cutting through the dark, oily-looking liquid with practised ease, its steady progress barely registering a ripple. Still I watch, transfixed, hypnotised by the animal's presence. Then, as fleetingly as it appeared, it lifts its body and vanishes – plop – into the depths of the Tyne.

There are some creatures which, no matter how often you see them, and however brief the encounter, leave you breathless with excitement. Sharing space and time with an otter, even for a few short moments, is an extraordinary privilege, and well worth getting cold feet for. Even several minutes afterwards I am still replaying every moment of it in my mind, a fading vision of an animal utterly at home in its watery surroundings.

Very few people have ever seen a live otter outside a zoo, but I suppose that, like the kingfisher and golden eagle, two other creatures whose reputation is certainly not based on familiarity, the otter's charisma outweighs its invisibility.

The British have always had a special relationship with otters. We have long admired them for their grace and beauty, especially when they hunt underwater, twisting and turning to and fro in pursuit of fish. They are one of the few species of aquatic animal equally at home both in and out of the water; unlike seals, which look so awkward when ashore, otters often travel across land to get from one river to another.

Otters have suffered decades of persecution. Until the sport was banned in 1978, they were still being hunted with packs of specially trained otter hounds, while they also suffered from the dredging and straightening of many lowland rivers during this period.

But what really did for the otter was the widespread and indiscriminate use of agricultural fertilisers during the post-war era, which drained off farmland and ended up in our streams, canals and rivers. Together with the dumping of sewage and industrial waste, this lethal cocktail of chemicals rendered many of our rivers virtually lifeless, so that otters could no longer catch the fish they needed to survive. The otters' position at the top of the food chain meant that the chemicals they ingested accumulated in their bodies and eventually killed them, just as they did with birds of prey such as the sparrowhawk and peregrine.

At their low point in the late 1970s, otters were virtually extinct in England, and had disappeared from many river systems in Wales and Scotland as well. They sought refuge on our northern and western coasts, where they found a haven from poisoning and persecution, adapting to a tidal regime by hunting during the daytime as well as by night.

Today there are at least 10,000 otters in Britain. The majority, about three quarters of the total, are in Scotland, but there are healthy populations throughout England and Wales as well. Indeed, they have now spread back to every English county, having finally reached Kent in 2011. They are also colonising our cities, using the canal and river systems to travel through urban areas by night, when few people are around to notice them. Camera traps have caught footage of otters in the middle of Bristol, very close to a shopping mall, and they appear to be thriving in this urban setting.

So how did we go from having virtually no otters thirty years ago, to so many now? The biggest difference has undoubtedly been the banning of lethal pesticides such as DDT, together with an end to otter hunting and a concerted clean-up of our rivers.

The return of this wild creature – and many others – to so many of Britain's river systems shows that they are healthier than they have been for a very long time. That's because otters are what scientists call a 'key indicator species': if they are doing well, then so is the habitat in which they live. Thus a healthy otter population is good news for kingfishers, swans, dragonflies, water voles and all the other creatures that rely on these precious watery habitats.

Not everyone is quite so delighted that the otters have returned. Anglers blame them for a decline in fish stocks, pointing out that a big dog otter needs to eat about 2 kilos of fish every single day. Otters sometimes raid garden fishponds, and have been known to feast on prize carp worth many thousands of pounds. In a way this is inevitable: when any animal returns after such a long absence it is bound to give rise to conflicts; but overall most people are glad to see the otters back.

❀

ONE OF THE reasons the otter is doing so well on the Tyne is that following the turnaround in the river's fortunes, the king of fish – the Atlantic salmon – has returned.

The salmon really is one of the great miracles of nature, both for its incredible athleticism and for its complex and finely balanced life cycle. Along with the eel the salmon is one of the very few creatures equally comfortable in both fresh and salt water. A fully grown salmon – they can reach 1.5 metres long, and tip the scales at up to 50 kilos – is a truly magnificent beast. It can leap twice the height of a human being, lay up to 7,000 eggs in a single spawning, and swim hundreds of miles out into the open ocean, before finding its way home.

Baby salmon begin their life in the upper reaches of a river such as the Tyne, where they hatch out from tiny eggs deposited in the silt along the river bed. The vast majority of the thousands of tiny salmon born here – known as fry – will die well before they reach adulthood. That's because they are the favoured food of a whole range of river creatures, including fellow fish such as trout, as well as kingfishers and even adult salmon, which will turn cannibal given any opportunity to do so. Those that do survive may spend several years upstream feeding on tiny aquatic organisms, and later, as they grow larger and are known as parr, on insects, crustaceans, tadpoles, and the eggs and young of other river fish.

At this crucial stage in their development salmon need several key factors in place: cool, clean water; shady areas with tree roots, stones or other debris where they can hide from predators; and above all a constant flow of water to provide oxygen, which in turn supports the complex array of underwater organisms essential to the young salmon's development. Should any of these factors not be present – for example, if a riverbank is cleared of vegetation, the river is dredged or the waters become temporarily polluted – then the young salmon cannot survive.

But if they do, then when they are three or four years old, they change their behaviour completely, and head downstream. What compels them to do so remains a mystery, but through some deep, ancestral instinct they leave the comparative safety of the upper reaches of the river and travel all the way down to the sea. As they do so their bodies gradually adapt from a freshwater to a saltwater lifestyle.

Salmon don't simply stay offshore near the mouth of the river where they were born; they swim right out into the open ocean, travelling hundreds or even thousands of miles during the next few years. All this time they are growing rapidly, until they reach full adult size.

For the growing salmon, the sea is no safer than the river: they may be eaten by seals, sharks and other larger fish, or even end up in the net of a fishing trawler. But for the few that do manage to survive, one final change awaits. Something in their instinct drives them home: back across the ocean, into the mouth of the river, and all the way upstream to the place where they were born. They navigate by using their acute sense of taste, and as their energy ebbs, the memory of where they started life drives them on. They won't eat or rest until they reach their birthplace – or die trying.

This journey is incredible enough, but it is made even more so because to get to its destination a salmon must battle across huge physical obstacles, including weirs and waterfalls that appear almost impossible to overcome. Watching a salmon leap over a waterfall five or six times higher than its body length, using every ounce of energy it possesses, is a truly awesome sight. The sheer energy and persistence involved is mind-boggling, as is the athleticism, the equivalent of a human high jumper leaping over a two-storey house. In recent years we have given them a helping hand, putting in 'salmon ladders' that enable the fish to get over these obstacles in smaller stages; even so, the effort required remains immense.

For those salmon that do finally make it back to the place where their life began – a tiny fraction of those that left the river years before – there is one final act: to find a partner and to mate. At this stage in their lives they seem to know what awaits them: they have stopped feeding, and so after mating, and once the female salmon has deposited her thousands of tiny eggs, both male and female usually die exhausted, their life's work done.

If just one part of the salmon's complex life cycle goes awry, then the very existence of this mighty fish is put in doubt. Back in the post-war era, salmon faced a major threat: our rivers were simply too polluted with chemicals and sewage for the fish to survive, and so numbers fell dramatically.

Following the clean-up of Britain's rivers, salmon thrived; returning to places like the Tees, Tyne and Thames, from which they had vanished, and increasing in numbers in those smaller Scottish rivers which had largely escaped the fate of watercourses further south. Things began to look good; both for the salmon, and for those creatures – like the kingfisher, heron and otter – which depend on it for food. But then, a few years ago, salmon fishermen began to notice that numbers were inexplicably falling once again.

This time, however, there has been no single culprit, no one problem that we can focus on and improve. For as with so many of Britain's wildlife and their habitats, salmon – and the rivers on which they depend – are under threat from a slow accumulation of factors, assailing them from every side.

Many rivers, especially in Scotland, are being dammed to provide renewable energy through hydroelectric schemes – a laudable aim in itself, but not when it changes the very nature of the river, and prevents the salmon from making their way upstream to breed. More traditional issues, such as illegal poaching, are also a problem. But all these pale into insignificance when we focus on what happens to the salmon once they are out at sea.

Climate change is already altering the temperature of the world's seas and oceans, with rapid warming disrupting the delicate balance of life by causing some creatures to shift their ranges northwards. Overfishing is also a major problem – like any sea fish, salmon can get caught up in the huge fishing nets used by industrial trawlers, and die in their thousands.

But the biggest threat facing the Atlantic salmon is much closer to home and easier to see. Salmon farming is now one of the biggest industries around Scotland's coasts; and as a result salmon has gone from being an unimaginable luxury – the fish equivalent of vintage champagne – to a cheap, easily affordable meal. There are now fifty farmed fish for every one wild salmon, which means that when the two meet – as they do when the wild salmon move out to sea – they are susceptible to the many diseases and parasites carried by the farmed fish.

One of the biggest problems is a group of small marine parasites known as sea lice, which cling onto the skin and gills of the salmon. These occur naturally on the wild fish, but because farmed salmon are concentrated in such artificially high numbers these tiny creatures thrive. When wild salmon swim close to salmon farms, the lice inevitably attach themselves to these migrating fish, causing sickness and even death.

As with farming on land, we face some tough decisions regarding salmon farming. It brings many advantages: cheap food for the consumer, jobs in some of the most remote and economically deprived areas of rural Britain, and revenue in the form of taxes for the government. But just as with intensive farming on land, the costs are equally great: the potential disappearance from Britain of the king of fish, the magnificent Atlantic salmon.

One man, Bob Kindness, is doing his best to save the salmon on the River Carron in the Scottish Highlands. His scheme has two main parts: first, he catches female salmon just as they are about to spawn, and takes the eggs to raise himself. Whereas normally only a handful of baby fish would survive their first few weeks of life, he can release thousands back into the river, giving them a much better chance of reaching adulthood.

The second part of Bob's scheme involves the anglers themselves. He issues licences for salmon fishing, but ensures that any fish that are caught are put straight back. The revenue from the licences helps fund his salmon-rearing project: the anglers are happy, and so are the fish. What's more, it has worked: ten years ago there were virtually no salmon left in the River Carron, while now there is a thriving population.

This is an ideal model to be rolled out right across the country. Giving the salmon a helping hand at the most crucial stage of their life cycle, combined with encouraging sustainable fishing, is a pragmatic and workable solution. And by opening up what has hitherto been a rather exclusive pastime to the many millions of recreational anglers who currently do not participate, we could create a far more sustainable industry. This would then allow the owners and managers of salmon rivers to help the salmon – both for their own benefit, and for the fish themselves.

This, of course, would help not just the salmon but all river wildlife: for like the otter, the salmon plays a pivotal role in riverine ecosystems, as both a predator of, and prey for, dozens of different river creatures. The salmon is also crucial because it passes through so many different habitats, and needs so many different factors to be in place for it to thrive: clean and healthy rivers being just the start.

So by helping salmon, we know we are helping both the river habitat and all the other wildlife that lives there. If the salmon were to vanish from our rivers it would be a cultural tragedy too: the king of fish surely deserves better. This magnificent creature has come back from the brink of extinction once; we mustn't let it disappear again.

❁

AS THE SALMON drives itself upstream, it may pass another river creature. But this one lives here all year round, never straying from its linear, watery territory: the dipper. This unique bird is closely related to the wren, and indeed looks rather like a giant version of that familiar garden bird: stout and pot-bellied, with a cocked tail held at a 45-degree angle to its body.

But although the dipper is a member of that vast order of perching birds known as passerines, it behaves very differently from wrens, robins or thrushes. Unlike them, it has adapted to life in water; and not just any old water, but the fast-flowing rivers and streams of Britain's uplands.

You rarely see dippers in the south and east of Britain; they are birds of the wilder north and west: from Exmoor and Dartmoor through Wales and northern Britain to Scotland, including arguably the most scenic river in the whole of Britain, and one as famous as the Tyne for its salmon, the Spey. Nestled below the high peaks of the Cairngorm Plateau, Strathspey ('strath' means a wide and shallow river valley, as opposed to a glen, which is deep and narrow) is one of the best places to watch wildlife in Britain. Visitors flock here in their tens of thousands to see the ospreys at Loch Garten, probably the most visited bird nest anywhere in the world. There are also capercaillies, crossbills and crested tits in the pine forests, and golden eagles soaring overhead.

But for me, even with these rival attractions, it's hard to beat spending an hour or two sitting on the banks of the Spey and watching the antics of a pair of dippers. Like a cross between a thrush and a torpedo, they skim low over the surface of the water on whirring wings, perching on water-splashed rocks in the middle of the river, and bobbing up and down with the characteristic motion that gives the species its name.

To feed, the dipper plunges head first into the foaming waters, then half-swims and half-walks underwater, before emerging a short way downstream, like a rubber duck in a bath. This enables it to feed on aquatic invertebrates, such as caddis fly or mayfly larvae and water shrimps.

As I watch, the dipper emerges once again – this time with a beakful of food. It looks around, then heads like a bullet for the riverbank, uttering a sharp, metallic call as it does so. Having reached the bank, it disappears into a cavity just above the rushing river. I peer through my binoculars and can just make out four wide-open beaks poking out as the dipper feeds its hungry young.

The position of the nest, only a foot or two above the water, makes it very vulnerable to flooding, but with luck these well-grown youngsters will manage to survive. Soon they will join their parents on the rocks below, where they too will hunt for food using that well-honed submarine technique.

Whereas the salmon's complex life cycle and multiplicity of habitats makes it vulnerable to a wide range of threats, the dipper is very sedentary, so will thrive unless its river home changes suddenly and unexpectedly.

Sadly, that is exactly what happened in the 1980s, when our rivers were affected by acidification.

Water running off from conifer plantations alongside rivers changed the pH of the river water itself; while emissions of gases such as sulphur dioxide and nitrogen oxide from factories and power stations combined with water molecules in the atmosphere to create what became known as 'acid rain'. Gradually our rivers were becoming more acidic, killing off the tiny aquatic creatures that sustain larger ones such as the dipper.

Fortunately the problem has now largely gone away. This was thanks to concerted international effort, including treaties to limit the emissions from coal-fired power stations, together with a switch over to cleaner energy sources such as solar and wind power. Today, the dipper is once again thriving on many of our upland rivers. On a bright, clear day in midwinter you may even be lucky enough to hear its characteristically rapid, thrush-like song; a sound that tells you that the river is in good health – for the moment, at least.

✿

BUT WHILE ONE sedentary river bird appears to be thriving, at least for now, another is facing more troubled times. The kingfisher is the James Dean of the bird world: it lives fast and dies young. Kingfishers rarely survive past their second birthday, and many die well before then, while the highest-recorded lifespan for a kingfisher in the wild is less than five years old.

True to its short span on this earth, a kingfisher lives its life at super-speed: whizzing up and down the river like a blue-and-orange bullet, and catching as many as a hundred fish every day to feed itself and, during the breeding season, its hungry brood. Barely the length of a sparrow, a fully grown kingfisher weighs just 40 grams – less than 2 ounces.

Like all sedentary river creatures, kingfishers are threatened by any sudden and unexpected change. Being so well adapted to their watery home, they can't seek refuge anywhere else – kingfishers can't survive in woods, gardens or the wider countryside. So they are always on a knife-edge.

As a predator near the top of the food chain, the kingfisher relies on a continuous supply of food, in the form of small fish such as sticklebacks and minnows. These in turn depend on smaller fish, amphibian larvae, insects and crustaceans, all of which makes them especially vulnerable to pollution.

Although our rivers are much cleaner than they used to be, thanks to laws against the once-standard practice of dumping chemicals and sewage into them, one-off incidents still occasionally blight Britain's waterways. It only takes a few moments for chemicals to be accidentally or deliberately released into a river, and then flow downstream, killing everything in their wake, as happened in the River Crane, near the famous Twickenham Rugby Ground in West London, a few years ago.

Our unpredictable weather, too, has an effect on kingfishers. A single harsh winter, with prolonged spells of ice and snow, can wipe out up to 90 per cent of the population; while summer droughts and downpours are equally unwelcome, as they too can reduce the food supply or flood the birds' nests. Climate change is already leading to more extreme weather events and unpredictable seasons, both of which are likely to cause problems for kingfishers.

Saving a bird such as the kingfisher is not straightforward, given the many and varied threats it faces. Keeping our rivers clean, avoiding disturbance to riverbanks (especially during the breeding season) and ensuring that there are plenty of fish for these birds to catch and eat will all help. But when it comes to hard winters and summer droughts, there is little we can do.

❦

ANOTHER CREATURE THAT shares its watery habitat with the kingfisher – the water vole – is also facing huge problems. The water vole has a special place in the nation's pantheon of small mammals – perhaps only the red squirrel can rival it for our affections. This is odd, in some ways, because this plump rodent shares many of its characteristics with its close relatives the house mouse and brown rat, both of which rate highly on the scale of animals we love to hate. But Kenneth Grahame's portrayal of 'Ratty' in *The Wind in the Willows* has given the water vole a permanent place in the nation's affections.

Over the past couple of decades water-vole numbers have fallen by well over 90 per cent, and this once-common and widespread mammal has now disappeared from many of the riverbanks and waterways where it was a regular sight.

The water vole would surely have suffered some decline in the past half-century or so, thanks to the destruction of riverbank habitat, and the pollution of rivers that so affected the salmon and the otter. But without question the biggest culprit in its demise has been the North American mink, an alien creature whose presence in our countryside is down to two monumental pieces of stupidity: one the fault of greed, the other of naivety.

The story goes back to the late 1920s, when a consignment of these creatures was brought to Britain to be bred for their fur. Soon a mink coat became the ultimate fashion accessory for Britain's richest women. It was the perfect way of gaining the upper hand over their less fortunate peers, and one of the first examples of a term coined earlier in the twentieth century to describe the ostentatious public display of wealth: 'conspicuous consumption'.

During the following decades, apart from a brief interruption during the Second World War, mink farming grew and thrived in Britain. By the time the Beatles had their first number one, in 1963, there were 700 mink farms in the country, with a combined total of tens of thousands of animals. But mink are nothing if not resourceful, and they didn't really want to be turned into fur coats for wealthy women with more money than sense. So they did what captive creatures often do: they escaped. And like many non-native animals before them – most notoriously another import from North America, the grey squirrel – they thrived in their new home.

Soon the UK mink population had reached well over 100,000 individuals, more than ten times that of their close relative the otter. Indeed, many people who assume they have seen an otter as they glimpse a sleek, slender shape disappearing beneath the surface have actually been looking at the smaller, darker mink.

One reason the mink thrived was, ironically, because the larger otter, which usually dominates its upstart cousin, had disappeared from our river systems. So the mink ran amok, preying on mallards and moorhens, kingfishers and coots, and of course water voles. The voles were defenceless against the mink: not just because of the latter's predatory nature, but also because its smaller size enabled it to get into vole burrows that were too narrow for otters to enter. Water voles can avoid many predators either by diving into the water or heading into their holes; but the mink is able to do both, and so vole numbers dropped like the proverbial stone.

By 1998, Britain's water vole population had fallen to a low of fewer than 1 million animals – down from an estimated 8 million in 1930. Then, just when conservationists assumed that things couldn't get any worse, they did. This happened as the result of an act of monumental stupidity from a group of people who, given their aims, really should have known better.

One night in August 1998 a group of animal-rights campaigners broke into a fur farm in Hampshire and 'liberated' up to 6,000 mink from their cages into the surrounding countryside. Despite fears of being seen as condoning the barbaric practice of fur farming, conservationists spoke as one in condemnation of this thoughtless and destructive act, rightly calling it an 'environmental catastrophe'.

A spokesman for the Animal Liberation Front, who had carried out this act of mindless vandalism, was forceful in his response; claiming that their action was justified as the mink were going to be killed for 'fur coats that nobody needs'. That may indeed be the case, but he appeared wilfully ignorant of the devastating effect of the release not just on water voles and kingfishers, but also on a huge range of other river creatures in the surrounding areas. Astonishingly, the spokesman even claimed that 'as they are territorial animals, you're not going to get packs of mink running around for long periods of time. They're not going to wipe out entire species.'

Given the destruction a single mink can wreak on the ecosystem of a stream or river, they didn't need to. The actions of the ALF helped to consolidate the dominance of the mink in Britain's waterways, and nearly two decades later conservationists are still battling to eradicate it, by trapping and killing any they can find.

The good news is that thanks to a series of organised culls – supported even by the animal-welfare charity the RSPCA – the UK mink population is now in decline, though not fast enough to avoid the animal being with us for the foreseeable future.

There is one small ray of light in the water vole's story. The return of the larger and more dominant otter appears to have led to a reduction in mink numbers on many English rivers, while the water vole itself also has a secret weapon on its side. Being such short-lived creatures – like most small mammals they rarely live longer than a year or two – water voles breed at an astonishing rate, with a female being able to produce a litter of up to eight, as many as five times a year.

They need to reproduce rapidly, because even when water voles are bred in captivity and released onto our river systems, most die within a few days, falling victim to the panoply of predators for whom vole is a regular item on the menu. We can only hope that a concerted reduction of mink numbers, allied to a continued programme of river restoration and breed-and-release schemes, can finally reverse the trend, and begin to bring water voles back to the places where they belong.

❀

BUT AS ONE creature enters what appears to be a terminal decline, so another makes a comeback. Down in the depths of the Devon countryside, a creature not seen in the wild in England since the days of *Wolf Hall* is now at large: the beavers are back. And like any new arrival, they are evoking a range of responses from a guarded welcome, through nervous suspicion, to outright hostility.

Bewhiskered and buck-toothed, beavers were once found all over Britain. But they were ruthlessly hunted for their soft, dense fur – one of the best insulators in nature – and for a substance in their bodies called castoreum, once used as a medicine. This finally drove them to extinction here, probably some time during the reign of Henry VIII – though a handful of animals may have survived as late as the eighteenth century.

A population of these huge, aquatic rodents has been at large on the River Tay in Scotland since the turn of the millennium. And now nine animals – four adults and five youngsters – are roaming free in England, appropriately, perhaps, on the River Otter in Devon. No one knows exactly where they came from, but it's likely that a pair or two managed to squeeze through a hole in a fence from a collection somewhere in the area, or perhaps they were deliberately released.

Initially, there were fears that the beavers might carry diseases hazardous to humans, but having been trapped and given the all-clear, they are now safely back in the wild. For the next five years, the Devon Wildlife Trust has been charged by Natural England with the responsibility of monitoring the animals.

The aim is to measure the beavers' effect on local wildlife, water levels and quality, and their potential impacts on farming. The Trust is also keen to see how local people feel about living alongside beavers. So far the community seems happy to have these animals on their doorstep. Dairy farmer David Lawrence, who farms land adjoining the river, has given them a cautious welcome:

> I think we've got a really good opportunity now to spend a few years living alongside the beavers and seeing how we get on with them. So far they tend to keep to the riverbank, and being nocturnal they are not mixing with the cattle at all. Maybe as they move higher up the river in the next few years they might build dams, which could cause a few problems. But I'm sure it won't be anything we can't solve.

On a national level, although many people have welcomed the Devon beavers' reprieve, others are not so sure. Perhaps predictably, given their stated opposition to reintroduced species, the National Farmers Union (NFU) stands firmly on the other side of the fence, opposing any reintroduction because of concerns about the possible damage to farmland caused by their activities. Another group opposed to reintroducing beavers is that of Britain's anglers. The Angling Trust, the body representing fishing interests in England, talks of 'huge potential risks to rivers', including flooding, creating barriers to the upstream movement of salmon and eels, the erosion of riverbanks and an increase in pollution.

It's easy to understand their concern, and indeed that of the residents of nearby Ottery St Mary, who may be worried that one morning they will wake up to find their fields and homes underwater because of the beavers' activities. After all, it's hard not to think of those old Disney films, in which hordes of industrious beavers cut down trees to build enormous dams across Canadian rivers, creating vast lakes and transforming the landscape.

The good news is that the animals in Devon are European beavers, a completely different species from their North American cousins. They do build dams, but in shallow water, and on a much smaller scale. So although they will change the landscape, this will happen at a very gradual pace. The beavers on the River Otter have yet to build any dams at all, despite having been at large for up to five years.

Indeed, the evidence suggests that rather than causing flooding, beavers act as 'nature's engineers', helping to prevent floods by slowing down the flow of rivers, while studies have shown that rather than harming fish, beavers help them by providing sheltered spawning grounds and cleaner water. They also create more complex habitats for other river wildlife, such as amphibians, dragonflies, kingfishers and the endangered water vole. Moreover, European beavers – whose global population fell to just 1,200 individuals at the turn of the twentieth century – have now been successfully reintroduced to more than twenty countries without such problems arising.

Some of the confusion over beavers has arisen because of the perennial myth that they are carnivores. Perhaps this arose because of their huge size and weight (about the same as a medium-sized dog) or those fearsome teeth, but beavers are actually vegetarian, and would far prefer to gnaw on a nice, juicy tree trunk than on a salmon or cute baby duckling.

The ongoing debate about beavers – one that often produces rather more heat than light – has a political element too. While countryside pressure groups call for a cull of the beavers, they happily encourage the release of up to 35 million pheasants into the British countryside every year – a massive cohort of alien birds that together have a greater biomass than all other bird species put together. Despite the damage done to our native wildlife –

pheasants are known to kill slow worms and adders, for example – this is somehow not seen as 'interfering with nature', even though it quite patently is.

For a native British species, especially when we were responsible for wiping them out in the first place, there is a strong case for giving these lost creatures a helping hand to return. But when a creature like the beaver has been absent from our countryside for so long, should we be quite so welcoming? One superficially persuasive case against bringing back the beavers argues that because Britain has changed so much in the past few hundred years, beavers no longer 'belong' in our countryside. Yet as we have seen with other reintroduced species such as the white-tailed eagle, red kite and crane, wild creatures that have been absent for decades – or even centuries – can and do fit back into our modern landscape; and indeed often thrive not despite, but because of, the changes that have occurred since they were last here.

Back on the River Tay, there are now at least 150 beavers at large. So far, they do not appear to be causing any major problems. Indeed, the diversity of wildlife on the river appears to be increasing thanks to the new habitats they have created. They – and the beavers in Devon – may have arrived as the result of a happy accident, but now that they are here, they surely deserve our encouragement. For as a symbol of what we can do to restore lost native creatures to the British countryside, creating new habitats and attracting visitors eager to see them, the beaver is pretty hard to beat.

❀

OVERALL, RIVERS AND their wildlife are doing pretty well – at least compared with other threatened habitats such as farmland and woodland. But now one factor threatens to devastate not just our river creatures, but virtually all our wildlife and the places where it lives. The elephant in the room – a problem that, if we cannot solve it, may literally mean the end of the world as we know it – is global climate change. And nowhere are the effects of this already being seen more clearly than the ultimate destination of this and every other British river: the seas that surround our little island.

5

Beside the Seaside

Coast and Sea

The sea is everything. It covers seven tenths of the terrestrial globe. Its breath is pure and healthy. It is an immense desert, where man is never lonely, for he feels life stirring on all sides.

Jules Verne, *Twenty Thousand Leagues Under the Sea* (1870)

AN ARCTIC TERN swoops down towards me out of the clear blue sky, wings held back, head thrust forward to attack. I raise an arm to defend myself, but I'm too late: a bright red, needle-fine bill pierces my scalp, and blood begins to trickle down my face. Arctic terns one, humans nil.

But this momentary pain and alarm are well worth it, just to experience the wonder that is the Farne Islands. The boat journey from the little port of Seahouses may only take twenty minutes, but it has brought me, and dozens of other eager pilgrims, to another world. Here, the birds are definitely in charge.

Lying just a few miles off the coast of Northumberland, the Farnes have been described by renowned wildlife film-maker Alastair Fothergill as 'the greatest natural spectacle in the northern hemisphere'. I've certainly never been anywhere quite like this.

From April to August the islands are home to a uniquely spectacular seabird colony; unique, because nowhere else can you get quite so close – indeed, sometimes rather closer than you might wish – to quite so many birds. Nowhere else can you experience the natural world in quite such an immediate, visceral way – not so much birdwatching as total immersion. And nowhere else do you get the feeling that the natural order of things – in which birds are naturally wary of human beings, and usually fly away whenever we approach – has been completely overturned.

Our first landing is on Inner Farne, the most accessible of this little group of islands. A flat-topped lump of hard, volcanic rock, covered with vegetation, surrounded by a deep blue sea, and thronged with tens of thousands of seabirds. As I climb off the boat and walk up the narrow path from the jetty, my senses are assaulted from every angle. A cacophony of cackles, cries and piercing screams almost drowns out the human voices, while the smell is, to put it politely, unique. Wherever I look there are seabirds – guillemots and razorbills, kittiwakes and shags, puffins, gulls and terns – more birds in one place than I have ever seen before.

Having run the gauntlet of the tern attacks, I reach the top of the path. Inner Farne is barely half a mile long, so

I can walk all the way around the island in half an hour – at least I could, if I didn't stop every few yards: to observe a baby Arctic tern as it sits patiently waiting its parent's return, to watch the predatory gulls trying to snatch a Sandwich tern chick from under its parents' beaks, or just to stand still and try to take in the whole, hyper-sensory experience.

❀

BRITAIN'S SEAS ARE alive with wildlife: from the northern tip of Shetland, where gannets nosedive into the water like kamikaze pilots, to the Isles of Scilly, where the harsh calls of terns fill the air on warm, summer nights; and from the deep trenches of the Western Approaches, where whales, dolphins and porpoises gather to feed, to the shallow waters of the North Sea, where puffins fish for sand eels to take back to their hungry chicks.

Our seas are special to us for historical and cultural reasons, too. Britain is an island nation, with a maritime history second to none, and a love of the sea runs through our veins like salt water. Nowhere in the whole of the United Kingdom is more than 70 miles from the sea, and for many of us, a lifelong fascination with all things marine begins with childhood holidays at the seaside.

Like most Britons, I cherish vivid recollections of those precious summer holidays by the sea, a fortnight's break from the humdrum, suburban world where we lived for the other fifty weeks of the year. The beaches were always sandy, the sun always shining, the ice creams always perfect – at least that's what my unreliable memory tells me, having erased the wet weather and boredom that I'm sure I endured at the time. Most vividly of all, I recall that the view stretched out all the way to the horizon, hinting at limitless possibilities beyond; again, a far cry from the hemmed-in views of semi-detached houses I was used to.

Yet our relationship with the seas around our land is both more complex and more paradoxical than this nostalgia would suggest. Beyond the coastline, which acts as a safety fence separating the familiar from the unfamiliar, lies the open sea. This is a place of danger, fear and mystery: a hidden kingdom surrounding our nation, at once part of us and yet entirely separate – out of sight, and often out of mind. Perhaps because of this disconnection, we have allowed even more environmental damage to happen in our seas than on land; which, given how bad things have been on land, is a pretty damning state of affairs.

But although for us the high seas – beyond both the horizon and our limited, terrestrial imagination – are an alien, unfamiliar world, for the birds they are familiar territory. Watching the seabirds here on the Farnes, we need to remember that this is exactly what they are: *sea*birds. They do come to land, but only for a few months each spring and summer, to lay their eggs and raise their young, before returning to their true home, the open ocean.

I take a few moments to think about the journey they will make when they leave these islands, in a month or so's time. On land, they are vulnerable to many dangers: being blown against rocks by wind and storms, having their eggs or chicks taken by predators, or being caught and eaten themselves by the fearsome-looking great black-backed gulls that loaf around on the edge of the colony, always on the lookout for an easy meal.

So while we usually think of the sea as a harsh, hostile and dangerous environment – which to us humans it often is – for these birds, it is home. It's a very safe home, too: seabirds live longer, on average, than almost any other group of birds in the world – some individuals survive for more than fifty years.

In just a few weeks' time, when their young finally fledge and are able to swim or fly, all these birds will leave the islands and head off to sea. For some, the journey is a relatively short one: the shag staring malevolently at me with his emerald-green eye as he tends his scrawny, reptilian chicks, will remain in the waters around the Farnes for the whole of the coming autumn and winter. Those guillemots and razorbills, squeezed cheek by jowl onto the narrow cliff ledges like bowling pins, venture a little further: as far as the Bay of Biscay, perhaps.

But the majority of birds here make epic journeys across the world's seas and oceans, with what seems like effortless ease. In August, as the breeding season comes to a close, the kittiwakes – poised, elegant gulls that constantly call out their name – travel not south, as you might expect, but north-west. They spend the autumn and winter in icy seas off the coasts of Labrador, Newfoundland and Greenland, where they may encounter their cousins from as far afield as Norway and Arctic Russia.

Puffins also make long and complex journeys, as scientists on the Farnes have recently confirmed by attaching tracking devices to the birds while they are in their burrows. They head first into the Bay of Biscay, then back and forth across the North Atlantic, before finally returning to their breeding colonies on the Farnes the following March, more than half a year after they left. During that time they will hardly have seen land, and not set foot on it once. Being at sea, of course, has its own hazards. If seabirds venture too close to land, autumn gales and winter storms can force them against coastal rocks, or in extreme cases all the way inland, in what is known as a 'wreck'. In the spring of 2013, following strong easterly winds, more than 3,500 puffins were washed up dead along the coasts of eastern England, while following the Great Storm of October 1987 dozens of seabirds turned up on reservoirs and gravel pits around London.

In the long term, though, the strategy of going to sea for more than half their lives makes perfect sense to the puffins. The real dangers facing this seabird – and many other marine creatures – are much more insidious, as we shall see.

❀

ONE SEABIRD HERE on the Farnes outdoes even the puffins' winter wanderings: that ultimate global traveller, the Arctic tern. Not that its tiny chick, crouched low in the grassy area to the side of the path, looks as if he'll be going anywhere soon. This tiny ball of fluff, buffish-brown speckled with black, could easily fit into the palm of my hand. And yet incredibly, before he reaches his first birthday, this little bird will have flown to the other end of the world and back.

He exercises his wings – little stumps of feathers, which I can't believe will soon grow into the aerodynamic wings sported by his parents – while uttering a persistent, cheeping call to attract their attention. Close by, an older chick is beginning to moult into adult plumage, yet even he looks ill equipped to fly at all, let alone undertake the epic journey these birds have ahead of them.

In less than two months' time, as summer gives way to autumn, these Arctic terns will head away from our shores, flying south. They will enter the Atlantic Ocean, cross the Tropic of Cancer, and go past West Africa, past the Equator and Tropic of Capricorn, until they finally reach the iceberg-strewn oceans around Antarctica –

a distance of about 17,000 kilometres or more than 10,000 miles. There they will fly alongside wandering albatrosses, snow petrels and south polar skuas, land on ice next to chinstrap penguins and elephant seals, and take advantage of the short-lived profusion of food that marks the brief southern summer.

Then, around late February and early March, as the days shorten and the nights slowly begin to draw in, they will head back north, retracing their journey until they arrive once more on the Farne Islands in April, to begin their breeding cycle again. No other creature on the planet travels so far, or experiences so much daylight, as the Arctic tern. During its lifetime, a single bird may rack up a total distance of 800,000 kilometres – half a million miles. And they don't all take such a direct route: Arctic terns ringed in Europe have been recaptured as far away as Australia.

The Arctic tern sums up the paradox of our relationship with seabirds. No other group of wild creatures allows us such an intimate encounter as this; yet no other wild creature is quite such a mystery to us. One moment it is here, an all-too-tangible presence as it swoops down to attack me; the next it is gone, to a world I cannot even begin to imagine.

❀

HAD I BEEN born a few thousand years ago, though, I might have felt a deeper connection with these ocean-going birds, for my life would probably have depended on them. Before the early farmers cut down forests and began to cultivate the land, most people in Britain and north-west Europe lived around the coast and made their living from the sea – by harvesting its wild creatures. Incredibly, this prehistoric way of life is kept alive even today in a community on the very north-western edge of Britain, in the Outer Hebrides. Each year a boatload of men from the village of Ness, on the Isle of Lewis, travels to a rocky islet known as Sula Sgeir to gather young gannets, known as 'gugas'.

Having visited Sula Sgeir myself – I say visited, but given how hard it is to land, we simply circled this wave-splashed rock by boat – I can only admire the bravery and strength of these tough, resourceful men. They spend a fortnight each summer living on this lump of granite in order to catch their quota of 2,000 young gannets. Once caught and killed, the birds are then brought back to Lewis to be boiled in milk and served as a delicacy. However, the guga's salty, oily flesh is something of an acquired taste: 'like salt-mackerel-flavoured chicken', as writer Donald Murray has wryly observed.

This custom does have its critics: animal-rights groups have campaigned for what they describe as an 'insane and monstrous' practice to be banned. Yet for those of us who regularly eat factory-farmed meat, as the vast majority of Britons do, it is hard to point the finger of blame at the guga hunters. They are also keeping alive an important cultural tradition. The collecting of seabirds for food may have died out thousands of years ago elsewhere in Europe (apart from the Faroe Islands and Iceland), but it continued all the way into the twentieth century on the archipelago of St Kilda; a cluster of islands, sea cliffs and tall, rocky stacks way out in the Atlantic Ocean off the Outer Hebrides.

Ironically it is our own, modern lifestyles that are doing real harm to our seabirds: overfishing and man-made climate change, which result from our constant need for economic growth, are causing far more damage to the marine environment than any hunting could ever do, and threaten the very existence of birds such as the guillemot, kittiwake and puffin.

❦

THE ISLAND OF Noss is one of about 300 different islands, skerries and islets that make up the Shetland Archipelago. If you want to see a variety of Britain's seabirds, amongst breathtaking clifftop scenery, then Noss is the place to come. As on the Farne Islands, it's not so much that you go to see the birds, rather that they come to see you. And just as you run the gauntlet of Arctic terns when you disembark on Inner Farne, so as you arrive on Noss you face one of the biggest, toughest and most terrifying seabirds of all: the great skua, known here by the Shetland name of 'bonxie'.

Chocolate brown in colour, with a fierce, hooked beak and black, beady eyes, a great skua looks and behaves like a gull on steroids. In flight they have a lumbering, awkward style: but don't be fooled, for when these birds go into attack mode they are fearsome opponents.

Bonxies nest on the open, grassy areas behind the sea cliffs, each pair marking out its territory just enough distance from its neighbours for them not to interfere with one another. But when you walk across the invisible line that marks the entrance to that territory, you immediately turn from a curiosity into an intruder. While one bird stays by the nest to guard the eggs or chicks, its mate takes to the air and circles around you, uttering a strangulated cry rather like a cross between a chicken and a crow.

At this stage, you might think that you will get away without being attacked, but if you do, you are sadly mistaken. Once the bird has gained enough height, it turns and heads straight for you, with only one mission in mind: to drive you as far away from its nest as possible. As it gets closer, you appreciate just how big an adult great skua is: weighing several pounds, and with a wingspan of almost 5 feet, this truly is a formidable adversary.

Locals tell you to carry a stick (or if you have one, a tripod) above your head, so that the bonxie aims at this instead of you. A few years ago a woman wrote to the *Shetland Times*, saying that this might hurt the poor birds, and suggesting carrying a stick of rhubarb instead.

Shetland isn't the easiest place in Britain to purchase rhubarb, and besides, I suspect a flying bonxie would make short work of any organic substitute for a hard stick.

Great skuas have a rather negative reputation, and not just because they attack us. They are what scientists call kleptoparasites, regularly chasing other seabirds such as kittiwakes and terns to force them to regurgitate their latest catch, providing the skua with a convenient takeaway meal.

But a few years ago, something strange happened on Shetland. Great skuas do occasionally prey directly on smaller seabirds rather than simply taking their food, and are also opportunistic scavengers. But many observers reported seeing the skuas attacking guillemots and other seabirds far more regularly than usual, while other birds were abandoning the coast each evening and instead patrolling Shetland's roads, looking for roadkill such as rabbits.

Whether this was simply opportunism, or a permanent shift in their diet caused by the rapid decline of the seabird species they usually rely on for food, it may be too early to say; but as with any change in behaviour from a top predator, it should give us cause for concern. Even more so, perhaps, given the global importance of the great skua population here in the UK, and especially in Shetland. For this is a truly scarce bird: there are just 16,000 breeding pairs in the whole world. Almost two thirds of these are in the UK, with about half in Shetland, so any problems faced by the great skuas here could be very serious indeed.

Ironically, their numbers have recently been rising, but this may be because in the short term the skuas are able to take advantage of the stress faced by other seabirds, as they in turn face major food shortages. As these birds' decline accelerates, however, the fate of the great skua could hang in the balance.

❀

THE GREAT SKUA isn't the only seabird facing problems. Britain's unofficial favourite seabird, the puffin, is in big trouble too. Even people who have never seen a puffin in the wild know exactly what these charismatic birds look like, thanks to fluffy toys, cartoon characters and for those of my generation and earlier, Puffin Books. In real life, puffins are rather smaller than you might imagine – about the size and shape of a bowling pin – with a plump body, black-and-white plumage and that extraordinary multicoloured bill, which earned them the name 'sea parrot'.

They have a comical waddle, making them look rather cuddly, which they most certainly are not. As those who put metal rings on the legs of puffins can attest, these birds have a vicious side; able to inflict a nasty gash with the sharp and powerful claws they use to dig out their underground nesting burrows. They also have a bizarre and unforgettable call: a low, moaning sound remarkably reminiscent of the extraterrestrial character ET, and as unexpected and amusing as the birds themselves.

The puffins which you can watch at such close quarters on the Farnes have experienced many ups and downs during the past decade, with numbers peaking at over 55,000 breeding pairs in 2003, then crashing by a third in 2008, when the census showed only 37,000 pairs. By 2013 this had risen slightly to just under 40,000 pairs: better news, but hardly cause for complacency.

Elsewhere in the UK, things aren't looking quite so positive. Puffin numbers are well below the long-term average, especially in the northernmost colonies in Shetland. Their decline – along with falls in numbers of several other species including guillemots and razorbills – has been blamed on a combination of overfishing and global climate change. Both reduce the numbers of sand eels: small, silvery fish on which many seabirds, including puffins, depend.

Judging cause and effect is tricky, especially in such long-lived birds, whose breeding success often varies from year to year depending on short-term changes in weather and food supply. But it does seem as if rising temperatures in the North Sea are causing the abundant plankton – the tiny marine animals at the base of the food chain – to disappear.

In turn, this has caused the sand eels to head further north into cooler waters, away from the seabird colonies that depend so heavily on their presence. In their absence, puffins have been forced to feed on totally unsuitable substitutes such as pipefish, a long, bony relative of the seahorse that causes the young puffins to choke to death.

During the last decade, the number of seabirds that once thronged the cliffs around the Shetland Isles has plummeted, and in some cases the nesting ledges are almost devoid of life. In other colonies, the adults have faithfully returned each breeding season, but because of a shortage of food have failed to produce even one chick between them.

One of the advantages seabirds have over, say, songbirds is that being so long-lived they are able to withstand a run of poor breeding seasons. The downside is that if the root causes of this lack of breeding success are not reversed, populations may appear to be stable for ten or twenty years, but then plummet as the older birds die off without being replaced by newer generations.

Those most affected by this problem include three of our commonest marine species: the guillemot, kittiwake and fulmar. Between them, these make up about half of all our breeding seabirds, so any major declines for these birds would be catastrophic for our marine ecosystem as a whole.

Not every species of seabird is in decline: larger species such as gannets seem to be doing rather well. That's because they do not feed on smaller fish such as sand eels, but on larger species, including mackerel and herring, which after years of decline caused by overfishing are finally making a comeback. But given the fragile state of our seas, and the seeming unwillingness of politicians to deal with the twin problems of overfishing and climate change, for how long will any of our seabirds continue to survive? There will come a point at which the equilibrium of this delicate and complex ecosystem will not return to normal; the tipping point beyond which the food sources will not bounce back. If and when this does happen, we will not just lose a few seabirds – we will have lost one of the greatest wildlife spectacles we have here in the British Isles.

❀

CLIMATE CHANGE IS having another effect on our marine life: bringing species we have rarely, if ever, seen before around our coasts. Leatherback turtles, basking sharks and fin whales – the second largest creature on the planet – are now regularly sighted in our offshore waters, as are about two dozen different kinds of whales, dolphins and porpoises.

Ironically, though, despite the rise in the number of individuals and species seen, these marine mammals are under greater threat than ever before. One reason for this is that our coasts and shores are home to far more human activities than they used to be. From windsurfing to waterskiing and snorkelling to scuba diving, our seas are increasingly crowded with people, causing all sorts of problems for our marine wildlife.

Disturbance is one issue; which is ironic, given that the very act of taking people to watch these animals might itself be part of the problem. Official marine and coastal ecotourism operators follow a clear code of conduct, meaning that they do not approach the animals too closely; yet other casual boat-owners may not be so scrupulous, or may simply fail to understand that their very presence can disturb the dolphins, interrupting their feeding or breeding behaviour. In the worst cases, a marine mammal may even be involved in a collision with a boat, resulting in injury followed by a slow, lingering death.

Fishing is also a problem: dolphins and porpoises compete for the same dwindling food resources as commercial fishermen, so can easily be caught up in the nets of trawlers and drowned. Then there is pollution: just as seabirds suffer when there is an oil spill or discharge at sea, so cetaceans, right at the top of the food chain, may also ingest these lethal oils and chemicals. The same applies to plastic: the large pieces of floating litter which they mistake for food, and the billions of tiny plastic beads now found in all the world's seas and oceans, which the animals consume without even realising it.

But perhaps the most serious issue is noise. Dolphins communicate by using a sophisticated system of clicks, buzzes and whistles – arguably the closest to human language in the whole of the animal kingdom. These complex sounds are used as an echolocation tool to help the dolphins find their prey, and also to communicate between different members of the same extended social group.

The increase in commercial and private boat traffic around our coasts – especially in our two main hotspots for bottlenose dolphins, Cardigan Bay in West Wales and the Moray Firth – is causing the animals more and more stress. In noisy environments, they have to 'raise their voices' to communicate with one another, just as we need to speak more loudly when there is extra background noise from road traffic or aircraft passing overhead.

This particularly affects mothers and their offspring, as they remain in shallow seas just offshore when the calves are young, to keep them safe while the female hunts for food. There tend to be more boats in shallow waters, so this creates a greater problem at this crucial time in the baby dolphin's life. Scientists and conservationists are now using sophisticated equipment such as underwater hydrophones to monitor the effects of increased noise on dolphin populations, but as these animals spend so much time way out of our sight, we can only catch the occasional glimpse into their complex lives.

When we do see them, it's often because they are in trouble, having accidentally been beached on the shore. But why do these highly intelligent animals – so well adapted to a life at sea – become stranded in the first place? Many different theories have been proposed to account for these catastrophic events, including bad weather, sickness and injury, or simply losing their way.

This raises a crucial question: if they have somehow become disoriented and confused, why should this happen? One theory is that the animals' navigation systems are being affected by sonar, used by the Navy to communicate both between ships and from ship to shore. Sonar works by sending out a regular pattern of sonic waves, which can travel through the water for hundreds of miles. There are several instances of marine mammals being stranded at a time when we know that naval sonar was being used in their vicinity, suggesting that the waves may somehow be affecting the animals' ability to navigate or communicate with one another.

The worst case of mass stranding in the UK occurred on the morning of 9 June 2008, at Porth Creek near Falmouth in Cornwall. A pod of more than thirty common dolphins had come ashore, and although the local lifeboat managed to rescue seven of them, the rest perished. Hardened crew members spoke of their distress at hearing the desperate cries of the stranded dolphins, yet being unable to help more than a few of them get back to the open sea. Later, a scientific report into the incident concluded that the stranding was 'most probably' due to the effects of sonar from a naval exercise involving over thirty different vessels taking place offshore. The theory was that the dolphins had initially headed upriver to flee from the noise, and then panicked and flung themselves onto the shore.

Post-mortems revealed that all the animals were in good health, with no sign of injury or disease, while weather conditions on the day were perfectly normal, thus ruling out any other likely cause for the stranding. Naturally, the Royal Navy denied that they were even partly to blame. But if we are to avoid such disasters in future we really must take a close look at the way we use military sonar, especially around coastal areas where dolphins and other cetaceans are known to live.

What is so worrying about an incident such as this – and all the other factors that may be impacting on marine mammals around our shores – is that ultimately we just don't know whether our marine wildlife will be able to adapt to these changes and maintain their populations. Whales, dolphins and porpoises are by definition 'apex predators' – those at the very top of the food chain. If our actions end up removing them from the marine ecosystem, the consequences are terrifying to contemplate.

❀

WE MAY CHOOSE to ignore the sea for much of the time, but we cannot always do so. Sometimes, the sea comes to us, impinging on our land-bound lives through onshore gales bringing death and destruction, storms breaching sea walls and flooding coastal homes and fields, or man-made catastrophes such as oil spills and tanker disasters.

Many of these one-off events are firmly lodged in our national consciousness. The devastating coastal floods of January 1953, which killed almost 500 people in Britain (and almost 2,000 in the Netherlands) and made thousands homeless. The oil tanker *Torrey Canyon*, which ran aground off the Isles of Scilly in March 1967, and caused devastation to holiday beaches and breeding seabirds. And most recently, the winter storms of 2013–14, so severe they swept the London-to-Penzance railway line into the sea at Dawlish in Devon.

As destructive as these one-off disasters are, however, the damage they do is far outweighed by events that go unnoticed by the media, as oil tankers accidentally – or deliberately – empty their tanks far out to sea. In February 2013, walkers along the World Heritage Site of the Jurassic Coast in Dorset were horrified to find the bodies of hundreds of dead and dying seabirds, washed up onto the shingle shoreline. The birds – mainly guillemots and razorbills returning to the local cliffs to breed – were covered with a sticky substance. When they were taken to the local RSPCA rescue centre, this proved obstinately impossible to remove with washing-up liquid, the usual treatment for oiled seabirds.

That's because this wasn't crude oil or diesel, but polyisobutene (PIB), a lubricant used to improve the performance of ships' engines. Hard though it is to believe, when ships are washing out their tanks they are legally able to discharge this lethal substance into the sea. By May, wildlife charities estimated that more than 2,000 birds of about 20 different species had died. The actual death toll was undoubtedly far higher, as many thousands of birds would have perished, unseen, in open waters.

Because incidents like this happen at sea, beyond our vision and our consciousness, they go unstopped and unpunished. Yet it's not hard to imagine the outcry if tanker drivers regularly dumped their waste chemicals into a village pond. Once again, we seem powerless to act against environmental threats beyond our shores.

⚜

NOT EVERY MARINE story, however, is a tale of woe and disaster. Our largest breeding mammal has, during the century since it was first given official protection, done rather well. But there have been many ups and downs along the way, and the story reveals much about the conflicts we face, as we try to find a balance between the competing interests of people and wildlife along our coasts.

The creature in question is the Atlantic grey seal, the larger and commoner of the two breeding seal species in Britain. A big male can weigh almost half a tonne – more than twice as much as our largest terrestrial mammal, the red deer. The grey seal is also one of the most globally important of all our mammal species, with almost half the world's population found around our shores.

Unlike any other British mammal, grey seals choose to produce their young at one of the toughest times of year – during the late autumn and winter. As storms and gales ravage the coast, the females haul themselves out on remote shorelines. Each gives birth to a single pup covered with soft, white fur, and then suckles it for several weeks on some of the richest milk in the animal kingdom. During this whole period she does not feed at all, instead living on her own dwindling fat reserves.

If the pup survives – and many do not, especially if their birth coincides with severe gales – then at just three weeks old its mother will abandon it. Soon afterwards, driven by the desperate instinct to find food, it will brave the sea for the very first time in its short life.

The grey seal has another claim to fame: it was the first mammal anywhere in the world to be given official legal protection, just before the outbreak of the First World War in 1914. The Grey Seal Protection Act set a close season from 1 October to 15 December, to allow the females to give birth and raise their pups. This ended centuries of killing and persecution, which had been carried out partly to obtain food and fur, and also because seals were regarded as competing with fishermen for their catch. At the time, it was thought that just 500 seals remained; scientists now believe there were perhaps a couple of thousand. Nevertheless, the species was clearly in trouble. Legal protection came in the nick of time, and worked very well indeed: numbers have since risen to at least 200,000 individuals.

You might think that this is a rare success story amongst a long catalogue of declines and problems for our coastal and marine wildlife – and you'd be right. But in the century since the grey seal was first given legal protection, progress has been far from smooth. For the grey seal was in many ways a victim of its own success, creating conflicts that could not have been foreseen when the legislation was originally passed.

Almost as soon as the grey seal was protected, and numbers began to rise again, so fishermen around our coasts protested that these animals threatened their livelihoods. Over the next few decades a number of schemes were proposed to reduce seal numbers – schemes that with the benefit of hindsight we might regard as crazy, but which at the time were taken perfectly seriously.

These included a plan to bomb seals from seaplanes as the animals slept on rocky islets in the west of Scotland; a proposal by fishermen on the River Tay to lay landmines on sandbanks to blow the seals sky high; and most bizarrely of all, a suggestion that RAF pilots should use the basking seals as target practice for their machine guns.

By the 1950s, with such outlandish schemes long since abandoned, a more serious attempt was made to lobby the government to control what fishermen described as the 'seal menace'. In 1958, the Ministry of Agriculture,

Fisheries and Food began the first official cull of seal pups. Controversially, this included those breeding on nature reserves such as the Farne Islands.

The public response was immediate and explosive. Newspapers ran emotive headlines such as 'Murder in the Nursery', comparing the baby seals to fluffy toys and calling for an immediate end to the killing. Yet during the following two decades the culling continued, until things finally came to a head in the late 1970s – thanks to a combination of political pressure at home and events thousands of miles away, on the pack ice of Arctic Canada.

Dr Rob Lambert of the University of Nottingham has studied the fate of the grey seal during the century since it was first protected. He believes that the reason the cull came to an end was ultimately down to a single image: a photograph of the legendary actress and animal-rights campaigner Brigitte Bardot with her arms around a fluffy white baby seal, which appeared in March 1977.

No matter that the seal in question was not a grey seal, but a North American harp seal, which at the time were being clubbed to death in their hundreds on Canadian ice floes; the picture still had the desired effect here in Britain. The killing of any baby seals rapidly became a flagship issue not just for conservationists and animal lovers, but also for the general public all around the world.

The RSPCA campaigned vociferously for the end of seal culling worldwide, while campaigners continued to highlight the plight of seals not in some remote part of the Arctic, but much closer to home: on the wildlife sanctuary of the Farne Islands. In March 1979, a rally was held in Trafalgar Square to protest against the killing, and comedian Spike Milligan even offered to parachute onto the Farnes to stop the cull. Sadly for posterity he never managed to achieve his ambition.

In the face of such overwhelming public opinion, it was only a matter of time before the cull came to an end. Even though limited killing of seals continued until 1985, the conservationists had won an important battle against commercial interests; one that prefigured the protests against badger culling almost thirty years later. But has the problem between grey seals and fishermen gone away? Hardly, especially given that making a living from commercial fishing has become more and more difficult in the intervening decades.

Ironically, many former fishing boats are now used to ferry tourists to watch seals in places such as North Norfolk, the Isles of Scilly and the Farne Islands themselves. This has been dismissed by some sceptical locals as 'city folk gawping at vermin', but like whale and seabird watching it undoubtedly provides an important economic boost to many coastal communities. Seal rescue centres are also thriving, and attract thousands of visitors keen to get close to these charismatic creatures.

That word 'charismatic' should perhaps give us pause for thought. Environmental historian Rob Lambert certainly subscribes to the view that if seal pups weren't so cute and fluffy, we might not have been quite so keen to save them from being culled. This combination of an innocent-looking, defenceless creature being beaten to death by a powerful human being triggered an emotional response from millions of people, the like of which may never be seen again. As he points out, we search for something essentially human in any wild creature, and the seal pup cloaked in white fur, with wide eyes and a vulnerable appearance, is a potent symbol of baby-like innocence, and one with which we readily identify.

The reality is, of course, that grey seals do compete for dwindling fish stocks and, in the absence of sustained hunting, numbers have exploded in the past century, to the inevitable detriment of fishing communities around our coasts. Yet to suggest that seals should be culled, even to a limited extent, would be a sure way for any politician to be forced to spend more time with their family.

In some ways it would be better for both us and our wildlife if we could manage our ecosystems – including intervention to reduce numbers where necessary – without worrying about the court of public opinion. But the situation will not, and in some ways cannot, change – when it comes to wildlife, emotion will usually hold sway over common sense.

But at least we can take comfort from the flipside of our widespread engagement with the fate of our wildlife and the places where it lives: that in many parts of the world such a concern would not even register on the political agenda. Only in Britain, perhaps, is a concern for our native wildlife so ingrained in our national sensibilities that, as has often been noted, we sometimes appear to care rather more for animals than we do for people.

And nowhere is this more so than in the setting of my next chapter on the ups and downs of Britain's wildlife: our towns and cities.

6

The Urban Jungle

Towns, Cities and Gardens

The park, the common, the high road: it wasn't an area
you could give a name to, or even a postcode; its borders
were too intangible for that. It was the rough territory of a
dog fox; the distance an old lady with a stick could cover
in an afternoon; the area a small boy could come to know
and call his own.

Melissa Harrison, *Clay* (2013)

THE LAPWINGS FEEDING on the exposed mud were
clearly agitated. Something was bothering the flock, and
for a moment I couldn't work out what.

Lapwings are edgy birds at the best of times, but these
smart waders, resplendent in their newly moulted dark-
green-and-white plumage, were even more anxious than
usual. When feeding they are constantly on the lookout
for danger; but today's nervous tension was unmistakable,
seeping into the autumn air like morning mist.

Then it happened. From out of nowhere, a dark,
purposeful shape appeared on the very edge of my vision.
Something about its strength and directness triggered an

image lodged in the depths of my memory, and I heard the single word 'PEREGRINE!!!' echo around me, as if being played in slow motion through a very loud amplifier.

It took me a moment to realise that it was I who had shouted the word, even before I had time to lift my binoculars and confirm the bird's identity. Fortunately, my first instinct was correct, and my fellow birders and I watched awestruck as this streamlined predator shot through the flock of lapwings when they took to the air.

Reaching speeds of almost 250 miles per hour in its hunting dive – known as a 'stoop' – a peregrine is one of the most impressive sights in nature. On this occasion, despite twisting and turning in pursuit of the panicking lapwings, the falcon failed to make a kill. But today, more than thirty years after I witnessed it, the excitement of my first peregrine sighting still lives with me.

Where did I have this memorable encounter with a creature that is not just the fastest bird in Britain, or even the fastest bird in the world, but the fastest living creature on the planet? A Cornish clifftop? A marsh on the Norfolk coast? An estuary in the far north of Scotland? Although these might seem to be the quintessential places to experience this ultimate wild creature, on this particular occasion it was a rather different setting. I was standing on the bleak concrete causeway that bisects Staines Reservoirs, just below the main Heathrow Airport flight-path, on the western outskirts of London.

Thirty years earlier, my chances of seeing a peregrine in such a shabbily suburban setting would have been very small indeed. It would actually have been hard to see one anywhere in Britain, as these powerful hunters had been driven almost to the edge of extinction here. By the late 1950s and early 1960s, Britain's peregrines had reached an all-time low. Like other species of raptor they were always persecuted, but two factors had made things even worse.

During the Second World War, peregrines had fallen victim to wartime paranoia. The British government feared that those nesting on the sea cliffs along England's south coast were chasing and killing homing pigeons, which could be carrying vital messages sent from RAF aircrew shot down over occupied France. Accused of being 'in league with Goering's Luftwaffe', peregrines were systematically targeted and killed.

With the war over, you might expect that the situation would improve, but in fact things got even worse. The adoption of 'chemical farming' – the widespread use of agricultural pesticides and herbicides to kill off insects and weeds and boost crop yields – led to continued declines for many species of raptor, including the peregrine. Being right at the top of the food chain, peregrines suffered most from the concentration of these lethal chemicals, which not only killed the birds themselves, but also thinned their eggshells, so the chicks would never hatch.

Fortunately, a few peregrines did manage to survive in the more remote upland and coastal regions of Britain, and the species has since made a spectacular comeback. But not even the wildest optimists would have predicted that this quintessential bird of wild places would then choose to colonise a very different habitat: the hearts of our major cities.

Nowadays peregrines perch on the roof of the Tate Modern art gallery on London's South Bank, nest on the iconic Red Road Flats in Glasgow, and soar high over Avon Gorge in the centre of Bristol, as thousands of people pass by in the streets below, most of them completely oblivious to the birds' presence. Elsewhere, though, peregrines are being brought to our attention through the imaginative use of new technology.

In the middle of Manchester, hordes of eager shoppers throng to the January sales at the famous Arndale Centre, bustling in and out of Poundland, Topshop and Carphone Warehouse before collapsing exhausted in Greggs or Starbucks for a much-needed refuel. Some are clad in the replica football shirts of Manchester's two major clubs: the red of United and the sky blue of City. Later on, they may return to the nearby Exchange Square to watch a crucial cup match on the 'Big Screen', thoughtfully provided for those many fans who are unable – or unwilling – to pay the astronomical ticket prices demanded for entry nowadays.

But outside the football season, when otherwise the screen would remain blank, another spectacle appears.

A webcam showing a pair of peregrines nesting on Manchester's second-tallest building, the 118-metre (almost 400-feet) high CIS Tower, broadcasts live images throughout the breeding season to those watching below. These also appear on the World Wide Web, enabling anyone with Internet access, anywhere in the world, to watch exactly what is going on at the nest on a minute-by-minute basis.

Two hundred miles to the south-east, on the impossibly slender spire of Norwich's medieval cathedral, another nesting pair of urban peregrines has become equally famous. And the same is true in towns and cities all over Britain, from Bristol to Birmingham and Derby to Swansea, as conservationists realise the benefits of showing urban people such a spectacular creature.

When they chose to nest in our cities, the peregrines didn't know they would become international media stars. They still don't, only being concerned to find enough food for their hungry brood of youngsters; but in the meantime they have brought a taste of the wild into our humdrum urban lives. And by telling the world about these very special birds, organisations such as the RSPB are demonstrating – about as clearly as you ever could – the real value of urban wildlife: that it changes the lives of people.

❁

Until very recently, the whole notion of 'urban wildlife' was regarded as something of an oxymoron. How could wild creatures possibly even survive in our cities – amidst glass and concrete, brick and stone, roads, traffic and houses – let alone thrive? The answer is, of course, that nature and cities coexist perfectly well. Imagine looking at a typical British city from the point of view of a wild creature: a bird, say, flying over the heart of the metropolis. What would they see beneath them, and why would they even bother to stop, let alone make their home here?

One reason to stay would be that virtually all British cities – and many of our larger towns – are built on rivers: the Thames, the Tyne and the Tees, the Mersey and the Trent, the Clyde, the Plym, the Exe, and many more. For our ancestors, these rivers provided a vital means of getting goods and people in and out of the urban settlements, and with plenty of fresh, clean water to drink. For wildlife, as we have already seen, rivers provide much the same set of functions, as well as a route along which migrating birds can plot their course.

From the air, as our bird follows the river far below, Britain's cities look rather like the African savannah: open areas of grassland – parks, gardens and other areas of greenery – surrounded by clumps of trees. That's no accident. Our nineteenth-century forebears, who believed strongly in creating a green urban environment long before this became fashionable, planted thousands of trees in our cities. They did so because these created a better atmosphere, both figuratively and literally.

Trees brought a sense of the countryside into the city; reminding these newly arrived urbanites of the rural homeland they, their parents or grandparents had left behind. But these linear urban forests, neat rows of trees lining the streets of every British metropolis, performed an even more valuable function: helping to keep the air clean by absorbing pollutants through the surface of their leaves – a vital service in the early decades of urban living, as factories and chimneys pumped out acrid black smoke.

When our bird comes down to land, it is simply looking to fulfil its basic needs: food, water, a place to shelter and ultimately somewhere it can breed and raise a family. Again, cities provide everything it could possibly want. There's food, both accidentally and deliberately provided by us, in the form of household waste and the seeds and peanuts we put out for our garden birds. There's water: in the river and its surrounding tributaries, but also in lakes and ponds and garden bird baths. Places to shelter, roost and nest? Our parks and gardens are chock-full of trees, shrubs and bushes, and of course nest boxes, while even the city's buildings provide plenty of opportunities.

For plants, the city is a fertile habitat too. Buddleia – originally from the rocky foothills of the Himalayas –

evolved to grow in niches and crevices in rocks, virtually anywhere it can get a toehold for its roots. Our urban landscape offers countless opportunities for such an adaptable plant, and so every June our cities burst into colour as these purple, nectar-rich blooms come into flower, attracting a plethora of city wildlife in the form of insects, especially butterflies.

On untidy corners of waste ground, clusters of shocking-pink rosebay willowherb compete with rangy stands of custard-yellow Oxford ragwort; just two more of the countless wild flowers – many, like the buddleia, originally from abroad – that have adapted to life in our cities.

Buildings are important, too – and not just as nest sites for urban peregrines. They provide another advantage to city wildlife that we cannot see, though we might sometimes feel, especially during a summer heatwave. The increased surface area created by thousands of buildings absorbs the heat of the sun, and then releases it at night, leading to a phenomenon known as the 'urban heat-island' effect. As a result – especially in the extremes of summer and winter – cities are several degrees warmer than the surrounding countryside.

For plants, the urban heat-island makes the growing season longer; for birds, it means they lose less energy on cold winter's nights; and for insects, it allows them to emerge earlier at the start of the year and stay on the wing for longer towards the end. The heat-island effect may be bad news for commuters as they sweat on a tightly packed bus or Tube train, but for our urban wildlife it is a major asset.

Cities are also a microcosm of Britain's different landscapes, cramming a huge range of microhabitats into one small area. In his book *Nature in Towns and Cities*, the pioneering urban ecologist David Goode makes a useful distinction between two different kinds of wildlife habitat in our urban areas.

The first category, which he calls 'encapsulated countryside', refers to those habitats that were there before the cities grew and developed. These include features of the landscape such as hills, rivers and lakes – and, in cities on the coast, estuaries – as well as older habitats that, although they may have been shaped by human hand, nevertheless prefigure the coming of the urban sprawl, such as ancient woodlands, marshes, heaths and meadows.

The second category is more varied and therefore harder to define, and includes a wide range of landscape features and human artefacts such as canals, roadside verges and railway cuttings; cemeteries, urban commons and post-industrial sites such as gravel pits; and most exciting of all, entirely new habitats either restored and improved or created entirely from scratch – again, often on former industrial sites.

They may be diverse, both in terms of their origin and their wildlife, but they all have one thing in common: they were created by us. These are not, of course, unique to urban areas: roadside verges and railway cuttings, for example, can be found running through the countryside as well as the city, which is why I cover many of them in the next chapter of this book, 'The Accidental Countryside'.

But many of them are indeed to be found in our towns and cities, and together with those remnants of original, pre-urban habitat, provide vital refuges for the wildlife that lives alongside us. So as a result of this extraordinary diversity of habitats, far from being a pale imitation of the surrounding countryside, a typical urban area can boast a much wider range of wild creatures than any similar-sized chunk of rural Britain.

Our towns and cities are home to large and small mammals: deer, badgers and foxes as well as mice, voles and shrews. They support a huge range of insects, from bumblebees to butterflies and hoverflies to hawkmoths. And let's not forget freshwater and marine creatures, from frogs, toads and newts in our garden ponds to the seals and even the occasional dolphin, porpoise or whale that sometimes venture upstream in our rivers.

There are wild flowers – not just the common or garden variety, but exotic orchids hidden away on brownfield sites in the hearts of our cities. I've come across a cluster of purple-flowered early marsh orchids blooming on a disused tennis court in the shadow of Newcastle's famous St James's Park football stadium, far from their usual home in wet meadows or acid bogs. At the more esoteric end of the scale, there are mosses and fungi, lichens and liverworts. Indeed, it's hard to think of any major group of British wildlife that cannot be found in at least one of our great cities.

What these urban plants and animals all have in common is that they display a suite of characteristics that enables them to succeed where others might have failed: resilience, toughness, and the ability to exploit the smallest and least promising opportunity. The very qualities, indeed, which have driven evolution – both biologically, and for we humans, culturally – over the generations.

Many of these plants and animals were here long before humans colonised the land and created the cities; they are the relict species of woods, heaths and meadows, which have managed to adapt as their surroundings changed over time. But others – often the most visible and exciting species – are recent arrivals; which have either spread into cities from the outlying countryside, or arrived here thanks to a helping hand from us. Many of these, such as the fox and the peregrine, the gaudy flocks of ring-necked parakeets and the much-reviled street pigeons, have come to define nature in cities. And for many people they may be the only nature they ever see, lending these species an importance that goes beyond the biological and ecological and into the realms of human health, culture and society.

So if you think that because you live in a city you are somehow short-changed compared with those who live in the countryside, then think again. As David Lindo – aka the Urban Birder – says, 'Anything can turn up anywhere, at any time. So just look up!' Or, if you prefer plants and insects to birds, look down.

❁

CITIES, LEST WE forget, are primarily designed and built for people: the four out of five Britons who either choose or are forced by circumstances to live in urban areas. So when a wild creature does move in alongside us, it inevitably impacts on our lives.

Some do so benevolently, like the garden birds for which two out of three people in Britain regularly provide food. Others, though, arouse mixed feelings, with some people welcoming their presence alongside us, while others vehemently reject them. And of all the wild creatures that have adapted to living in our midst, one species polarises opinion more than any other: the urban fox.

Many of the creatures I have encountered since I have been living in rural Somerset behave in more or less the same way as those I left behind in the suburbs of London: garden birds, for instance, flock to feeders and potter about on grassy lawns whether they are in the city or the countryside. But the fox behaves so differently it might as well be another species, which when you consider that before the Second World War foxes were almost unknown in urban areas, is quite incredible.

The bottom of our garden is a sun trap, sheltered from the south-westerly breezes that blow almost constantly from the Atlantic across our village. It is the perfect place for a fox to have an afternoon nap: and one day I came across one, stretched out in the heat of the July sunshine. I got to within a few metres of her when she awoke and caught sight of me.

Having spent half my life in London, I was used to the insouciant attitude of the urban fox; an almost teenage surliness, as it looks down its snout with those piercing black eyes, defying me to share its territory. This fox could not have behaved more differently. As she awoke I saw the fear in her eyes, followed by the quickest departure I had ever seen, melting within seconds into the brambles and hawthorn scrub at the end of our garden.

Since then, I have come across foxes many times as I walk or cycle around the lanes of my country parish. Every time I do, even if I am several hundred metres from them, they turn and trot away in the opposite direction as quickly as they can. Foxes may no longer be (at least legally) hunted by dogs, but they are frequently shot, and having seen a fox make short work of one of our chickens I can feel some sympathy with my rural neighbours' hostility towards them. But despite this antipathy, no one would deny that the fox somehow 'belongs' in the British countryside. Indeed, it has long been celebrated by those who like nothing better than to chase it down with a pack of hounds.

In the city, people's attitudes towards foxes are both more ambivalent and far more polarised. Some feed them with the same dedication and love that they lavish on their garden birds. They welcome these predatory mammals into their private space, watching with undisguised joy and fascination when foxes choose to make their home beneath the garden shed, where they raise their undeniably cute cubs, which jump and play on fine spring days amongst the lawns and flower beds of leafy suburbia.

Others despise foxes as vermin, feeling nothing but contempt for those who lavish care and affection on what they regard as ruthless killers. No one living amongst city foxes can, it seems, remain indifferent to their presence. You either admire their confidence and chutzpah, when they don't even bother to cross the road as you approach; or you want every single urban fox to be culled, to eradicate this rural intruder from our city streets.

When Channel 4 ran their television series *Foxes Live: Wild in the City* in spring 2012, the contest between the defenders of the fox and their opponents reached new heights. While many viewers appeared to be spending their every waking hour following the GPS-tracked foxes, others were crusading for urban foxes to be wiped out. This won support from public figures such as the Mayor of London, Boris Johnson, who following an attack on a baby the following year firmly came out in favour of a cull, in a typically shameless attempt to court popularity.

This was not the first instance of a fox apparently entering a house and attacking a child: in the summer of 2010 two twin sisters were mauled by a fox in their bedroom in the London Borough of Hackney, an incident that hogged newspaper headlines and TV news bulletins for days. Horrible though such incidents are, they do need to be put in perspective. If foxes are entering people's homes, it is probably because someone in that neighbourhood has encouraged them, perhaps by hand feeding them on their patio.

Urban fox expert Professor Stephen Harris of the University of Bristol does not condemn the feeding of foxes per se – he has done so himself for many years. But he does counsel against treating these wild animals as substitute pets, and especially against inviting them into the home, thereby breaking down the barrier between them and us, which is crucial if foxes and humans are to coexist in our cities.

The other reason we should engage in reasoned debate about urban-fox attacks, rather than indulge in hysterical calls for their culling (which would be both impractical and unpopular amongst millions of animal-loving city dwellers), is that fox attacks are so incredibly rare.

Domestic dogs attack many thousands of people every year, with roughly 6,000 being bitten so badly that they seek hospital treatment, and an average of two or three a year (almost all young children) dying as a result of their injuries. Yet few people would call for a wholesale cull of our nation's favourite pet.

Myths abound about urban foxes: that they roam the city at night in packs like wolves, and that they are becoming not just bolder than ever before, but also bigger: reports of 'giant foxes' frequently surface in the newspapers, with no hard evidence ever being offered to support these claims. It is as if having wiped out the really big predators – the lynxes, wolves and bears that once roamed our land – we need some mythological beast to replace them in our fears and nightmares. In the absence of anything bigger and better, 'giant killer foxes' will have to suffice.

Some critics have suggested that the campaigns against urban foxes are driven by the vested interests of the pro-hunting lobby and commercial pest controllers, hoping to make money out of a cull. Yet I think this oversimplifies the situation, which is more deeply embedded in our collective psyche. In many ways, the fox serves as a symbol of truly wild nature in our cities: a symbol we either embrace as something to be welcomed and encouraged, connecting us with the wild world; or reject out of hatred, fear and prejudice.

The truth about foxes, of course, lies somewhere in between. Whatever we think of urban foxes does not change the reality: that these wild creatures have, partly through necessity and partly through opportunity, moved in alongside us and are getting on with their day-to-day lives.

They have done so by a rapid process of adaptation, notably by living at much higher densities than in the countryside. Whereas the territory of a fox in the Scottish Highlands may cover as much as 4,000 hectares (15 square miles), and even in rural lowland England a typical territory is between 270 and 520 hectares (roughly 1 to 2 square miles), an urban fox's territory may be as small as 8.5 hectares – less than one thirtieth of a square mile, or about the same size as nine football pitches.

Foxes have also taken advantage of human structures – many of their earths are under garden sheds or other outbuildings, and on sunny days they will often happily sunbathe on a garage roof. But in some ways they have not changed: urban foxes do occasionally raid dustbins, but contrary to popular belief this does not make up a significant proportion of their diet; just like rural foxes they are opportunistic feeders and will take what they can find.

If we step back for a moment from the debate, and instead look at them from an ecological point of view, it is obvious why urban foxes are here: our cities provide everything they could possibly need in terms of food, shelter and a place to raise a family. In some ways they are not so different from those human economic migrants who move into the city in search of a better life; and just like human migrants, they are welcomed by some and reviled by others.

❀

THE MOST UBIQUITOUS and obvious urban inhabitants, apart from us, are of course the birds. Not just the usual suspects – sparrows and starlings, finches and tits, pigeons and thrushes – but a whole range of more unusual species.

City trees ring with the drumming of great spotted woodpeckers, while our park ponds are home to coots and moorhens, and many different kinds of ducks, geese and swans. Some of these are local residents, rarely venturing outside the park gates, while others, such as the wigeons and shovelers that throng Hyde Park's Serpentine in autumn and winter, may have travelled here from as far afield as Siberia.

In the suburbs that ring the outer fringes of our cities, disused gravel pits host great crested grebes, playing out their elaborate courtship display on spring mornings to a select few early risers lucky enough to witness it.

Cities even have their own unusual species, not found at all in the surrounding countryside. In the heart of London, a sharp, metallic burst of song, rather like a bagful of ball bearings being rattled, signals the territory of a male black redstart. This modest little bird, looking rather like a robin covered in a layer of soot, colonised Britain during and after the Second World War, taking advantage of a wholly new and temporary habitat to do so. Black redstarts are common across much of mainland Europe, living on rocky hillsides or at the edges of towns and villages, where they have learned to exploit marginal habitats in places where other species find it impossible to thrive.

Their big break here came as a result of one of the greatest tragedies to hit modern Britain: the Blitz. The wholesale destruction of huge swathes of London by the German Luftwaffe created derelict sites covered with rubble, which mimicked the black redstarts' native habitat, providing the niche they needed to colonise Britain as a breeding bird.

Since the clearing and redevelopment of the bomb sites, black redstarts have moved to other places to breed, including famous locations such as the Millennium Dome, Canary Wharf and Wembley Stadium. They have also gradually spread north and westwards to colonise Birmingham, Manchester and Liverpool, where they breed in the disused docks. Being at the north-western edge of their range, they are helped enormously by the urban heat-island effect: the higher temperatures in cities – and the more insects they bring – may be what is tipping the balance between success and failure for this charming little bird. Sadly, though, the pressure to develop these brownfield sites, driven by the rising price of land and property, means that this charismatic species is now only just managing to hang on as a British breeding bird.

The story of the black redstart shows one ingenious way in which wildlife is able to colonise our urban areas: by finding what ecologists call 'analogue habitats'. To those birds arriving in Britain in the 1940s and 1950s, a derelict bomb site, covered with newly colonising plants such as rosebay willowherb and awash with small insects, was virtually identical to its natural home on rocky hillsides.

Analogue habitats like this have allowed three different kinds of birds, with very different needs and requirements, to colonise many of our larger cities. We usually associate them with other habitats and locations, places that seem a million miles away from the hearts of our cities. Yet these three types of birds have not just survived in the city, but thrived.

The trio is composed of what is perhaps the most overlooked bird in Britain, the feral pigeon; the fastest creature on the planet, the peregrine falcon; and, most recently, the group of large seabirds we colloquially call 'seagulls'.

❀

LISTEN TO THE opening bars of the theme music of Radio Four's *Desert Island Discs*, and I defy you not to be transported back to your childhood, to those summer holidays by the seaside. It's not the music alone that provokes this bout of nostalgia, but the presence on the soundtrack of the calls of one of our most familiar coastal birds: the herring gull.

Those harsh but strangely evocative cries, delivered as the bird throws its head back and opens its bill so wide you can almost see what it had for breakfast, is for many of us the trigger for a flood of early memories. Buckets and spades, sandcastles and saucy postcards, candyfloss and Mr Whippy ice creams – all the classic ingredients of a British seaside holiday.

Yet if you want to hear the sound of the seaside nowadays, you certainly don't need to travel far. Take a stroll down Oxford Street in London, Whiteladies Road in Bristol, or around Birmingham's Bullring, and above the noise of passing traffic you'll soon hear the cries of the herring gull, often accompanied by those of its slightly smaller, darker-backed cousin, the lesser black-backed gull.

Both herring and lesser black-backed gulls were, until very recently, primarily birds of the coast. They did venture inland, especially during autumn and winter, when they could be seen lounging around on playing fields, or passing overhead at dusk to roost on reservoirs and lakes. But when spring came, they would head back to the seaside, nesting in noisy colonies on cliffs and offshore islands, and following fishing boats to feed on the guts and other remains cast overboard by the crew.

In the past few decades, as the fleets of fishing boats plying their trade around our coastline have given up the losing battle of trying to make a living, fish are no longer being thrown into the sea. So with their main food source now gone, gulls have turned to alternative ways of getting something to eat.

Reports of children crying with fear and anguish as gulls swoop down to grab their ice creams have become all the more frequent. And rarely have I seen anyone so surprised as the man sitting on the promenade in the Cornish resort of St Ives who, just as he prepared to bite into his meat pasty, had it rudely snatched from his hands by a passing gull, leaving just the crusts behind.

Not that the gulls have been thriving on these stolen handouts. Their population has gone into a steep decline, and in 2009, the herring gull was added to the Red List of Birds of Conservation Concern, following a fall of more than half in its breeding numbers. Fortunately for the birds themselves, though not perhaps for the human inhabitants of our cities, they have discovered both a new and reliable source of food and an alternative place to nest and raise their families.

The food source came directly from us: the vast landfill sites that have popped up around the edges of many of our cities. They provide everything these adaptable and omnivorous birds can eat: vast piles of waste food, thrown away into our kitchen bins, then collected and dumped onto a veritable banqueting table for the gulls.

Ironically, given the way they blight our landscape with their sight, noise and smell, these landfill sites are the consequence of one of the most important measures ever taken to improve our natural environment: the Clean Air Act of 1956.

Before that date, most household rubbish was burned, with its fumes combining with the smoke from coal fires and winter fogs to create the infamous 'London Smogs' of the post-war period. These terrible events resulted in the premature deaths of thousands of people, and the chronic illness of tens of thousands more.

When the burning of rubbish was banned, virtually overnight, local authorities had to find a new way to dispose of it. They did so by creating landfill sites – or, as most of us call them, rubbish dumps. In the late 1950s, this must have seemed like a sensible solution to the problem. But as our consumer society grew and habits changed, leading to an exponential increase in the amount of food we throw away, more and larger sites were needed to deal with all our refuse.

On a winter's afternoon at the vast landfill site on the outskirts of the cathedral city of Gloucester, flocks of gulls fill the air like snowflakes, creating an undeniably impressive spectacle as they rise up into the air en masse to dodge the noisy earthmovers. As soon as the machines have gone past, though, the gulls drop swiftly down to settle on the huge piles of refuse below.

Deftly – as if it were dealing with a portion of fine food at a feast – a gull picks up a scrap of some unidentifiable piece of meat or vegetable, tosses it into the air and wolfs it down its gullet, followed by another, and then another.

It must be quick: if it hesitates for a moment, another bird will get there first, seizing the morsel literally from its beak. All the while the gulls jostle and squabble, uttering their warning calls to one another, even though from where I am standing it looks as if there is plenty of food for all.

As dusk begins to fall on this late-December afternoon, I rub my hands together in a vain effort to keep warm, hoping that the birds will call it a day. But it is almost dark before they finally do so, rising as one and flying off to roost for the night.

Throughout the autumn and winter, the gulls come here in flocks of tens of thousands to feed on this banquet of waste. But as the first signs of spring appear, their thoughts turn to raising a family. To do so, they used to head back to the coast, but in the past decade or so they have chosen a far more convenient place to nest; on the roofs of buildings in the cities that cluster around the Severn Estuary: Gloucester, Bristol and Cardiff. They are now well established in Central London, too: I can still recall the surprise I felt back in the late 1990s, when I heard the cries of a herring gull echoing above the Euston Road in May, the middle of the breeding season. Now, just two decades later, such a sound would hardly merit any comment.

Gulls have moved into cities not only because these places are closer to their main food source, but also because those that nest on roofs are much safer from predators such as foxes. As a result they raise far more of their youngsters to maturity than birds on the coast: usually two or three per nest, which has resulted in urban gull populations rising very rapidly indeed.

They can also feed and scavenge after dark, under the city lights – a particularly rewarding pastime on Saturday nights, when they supplement their usual diet with kebabs, burgers and chips dropped by binge-drinking revellers. One enterprising urban gull in Aberdeen even learned to enter a local shop and help himself to a packet of crisps. Nicknamed Sam, his fame soon spread, and eventually local shoppers started paying for the food he had taken.

Today, it has been estimated that as many as 150,000 pairs of gulls breed in urban and suburban areas of Britain, many of which are in any case – like Bristol and Cardiff – only a short distance from the coast. Given that until a couple of decades ago there were virtually no urban gull colonies, this shows just how adaptable these birds are. And having arrived, they have little or no reason ever to return to the seaside.

What worries many people, though, is that if the population continues to grow at the current rate, there could be well over 1 million urban gulls in just ten years' time. And that really could cause problems. City dwellers – whose usual encounters with nature are via their television sets or on their garden bird feeders – are not all enamoured of this bulky new arrival in their home territory.

Attitudes towards urban gulls vary from grudging acceptance at one end of the spectrum to a visceral hatred at the other, fuelled by a litany of national and local newspaper headlines about the horror of gull attacks. Herring gulls do have a wingspan of well over a metre, a fearsome bill at one end and a nasty habit of jettisoning a messy load from the other, so it's not surprising that people are frightened when dive-bombed by these formidable birds.

As with city foxes, there have been calls to cull urban gulls: either directly, by shooting or trapping, or indirectly, by removing their eggs, or covering them with a thin layer of oil which kills the unborn chicks. Less drastic solutions include using a falcon to frighten them away, though where this has been tried the gulls quickly get used to the presence of the predator, and then ignore it.

Another approach is to target not the gulls themselves, but us. A few years ago, the town council in the Suffolk seaside resort of Aldeburgh announced that they would impose a hefty fine of £2,500 on anyone who dared to feed the local gulls. And in the summer of 2015 a spate of attacks by gulls on humans (and the deaths of a pet tortoise and an unfortunate Yorkshire terrier) hit the headlines once again, even prompting Prime Minister David Cameron to call for 'a big conversation' about the gull problem.

I hesitate to confront the collective wrath of holidaymakers and city dwellers up and down the country, but one possible solution might be to learn to live with gulls. Setting our prejudices aside, they are some of the most graceful, beautiful and fascinating birds we are ever likely to see. Nobel Prize-winning scientist Niko Tinbergen certainly thought so: his pioneering observations during the 1940s of the behaviour of gulls led to the establishment of the science of ethology – the study of animal behaviour.

And if you need any more convincing that gulls are special, just head to the coast and find one of the few remaining breeding colonies. As the birds float overhead against a cobalt-blue sky, throwing their heads back and uttering that classic ringing call, they are momentarily transformed into one of the most beautiful creatures we shall ever have the privilege to see.

❀

GULLS MAY BE relative newcomers to our cities, but one species of bird has been with us for centuries, perhaps millennia. Yet feral pigeons – or London, domestic or street pigeons, as they are also often known – rival the magpie and sparrowhawk (and now, perhaps, the 'seagull') for the title of Britain's most hated bird. They can be found in every British town and city, going about their daily lives with what appears to be a cavalier disregard for their human neighbours.

Walk past a pigeon as it struts around on a crowded pavement or in a city square, pecking at the hard ground for morsels of food, and it might deign to dodge out of the way, or perhaps fly a few yards. But it will not behave as most other wild birds do: watching warily for every possible danger, fleeing with a loud alarm call, or simply keeping a careful distance between itself and any human passers-by.

As a result of its ubiquity and familiarity, we have in turn learned to ignore the feral pigeon. This is perhaps surprising, given the range of amazing things they do right under our noses: such as hitching a ride on the London Underground to get from one station to another, a phenomenon first observed in the 1970s.

In recent years London's population of feral pigeons has fallen slightly. This is partly because of concerted efforts to stop tourists feeding them (notably in Trafalgar Square, where feeding pigeons was banned by the former Mayor of London, Ken Livingstone), and partly because as older buildings are demolished and replaced by new ones, there are fewer places where the pigeons can make their nests. But they are still fairly ubiquitous in the built-up areas of the capital and in most other British city centres.

So where did feral pigeons come from in the first place? To find the answer, we must travel to the extreme north and west of Britain, to the sea cliffs of the Outer Hebrides, about as far from the urban jungle as you can possibly get. Hidden amongst this spectacular scenery is an ordinary bird with an extraordinary story to tell: the shy, reclusive rock dove.

It's not easy to get a close look at a rock dove: for they are flighty creatures. But if you do manage to see one well, the similarities between this bird and its urban cousin are remarkable. There is, however, one obvious difference: whereas street pigeons come in a wide range of shades and markings, reflecting their messy domestic ancestry, rock doves are uniformly identical to one another. They have a powder-grey head and body, a greenish shimmer on the neck, black wingbars, reddish eyes, and when they fly away – as they usually do when you get anywhere near them – a flash of white on the rump.

Hard though it is to imagine when you watch rock doves in their natural habitat, they are the ancestors of domestic and feral pigeons throughout the world. They were amongst the very first wild creatures to be domesticated, at least 2,000 years ago and probably earlier. Since then they have been used for food, to carry messages, and in the popular sport of pigeon racing.

But these birds cannot be easily confined to a cage or dovecote. So over the centuries many have 'gone feral' and established free-living colonies, finding a suitable substitute for their original homes in our urban environment, and becoming the quintessential city bird.

The reasons for the feral pigeon's success are in many ways obvious. They thrive on the creature comforts of our cities: takeaway food, plenty of water to drink and bathe in, and convenient city-centre homes in our old buildings. Yet instead of welcoming them for their adaptability and streetwise skills, we deplore them. Partly this is because of their habits, which have led them to be dubbed 'rats with wings'. But it might also be because they remind us of another highly adaptable species that has taken to cities rather well: us.

❀

UNTIL RELATIVELY RECENTLY, pigeons thrived in cities partly because their oldest enemy did not. But now that the peregrine has colonised Britain's urban areas so successfully, things have changed. So it's fortunate for Britain's feral pigeons that they are not the only item on the peregrine's menu. For urban peregrines – in London at least – have a marked preference for Indian takeaways, in the form of the most brash, exotic and colourful of all our urban creatures, the ring-necked (also known as the rose-ringed) parakeet.

No other city creature demands quite such a degree of attention as this incomer from India. Its loud, raucous call, emerald-green plumage, and habit of gathering in huge flocks, which pass over London's skyline each evening on their way to their night-time roost, all contribute to making this bird impossible to ignore. And yet almost half a century after they arrived here in the late 1960s, people are still sometimes astonished to see bright green parakeets flying around in the London parks.

The story of how they got here is fascinating; it is also the subject of some bizarre and wholly inaccurate speculation, and some extraordinary urban myths. The first regular sightings of parakeets in the London area date from 1969, though there is evidence that small groups were at large in parts of the capital a few years before this, and the very first London record (of a single escapee seen in Dulwich) dates back to 1893. The 1969 sightings coincided with the era of Swinging London and Flower Power, hence the widely held but sadly erroneous belief that they originated from a pair (named Adam and Eve) released by a stoned Jimi Hendrix from the window of his central London apartment. Another celebrity connection, with Humphrey Bogart, is even more tenuous: the parakeets are said to have escaped from the set of *The African Queen*, made at Isleworth Studios in West London.

Advocates of this latter story struggle to explain where these gaudy green birds managed to hide for almost twenty years, given that the film was made in 1951. What is far more likely is that the current population derives from the deliberate or accidental release of caged birds imported from their native India over a period of time.

Since their first arrival, the parakeets have thrived, and were finally accepted by the British Ornithologists' Union as an official British bird in 1983. Since then their numbers have risen from a few hundred to a current estimate of about 8,500 breeding pairs, with as many as 30,000 birds post-breeding. Numbers rose tenfold in just fifteen years from 1995 to 2010, making the parakeet the fastest increasing of all Britain's birds during that period.

And yet ring-necked parakeets are still largely confined to London and the surrounding counties. This is partly, perhaps, because the species roosts communally, and so tends to stay in the same area rather than expanding its range. Paradoxically, this means that in some parts of London, such as Richmond Park and Kew Gardens, the ring-necked parakeet is now one of the commonest – and certainly one of the most visible – birds.

The effect of the newcomer on London's resident species is not at all clear. Parakeets nest in holes, and although they struggle to squeeze into old great spotted woodpecker holes made by a bird barely half their size and length, they still manage to do so. Concerns that they might be displacing other hole-nesting species such as jackdaws, stock doves and nuthatches, and the parakeets' ability to cause damage to fruit trees and other crops, have led to calls for a cull, and in 2010 the species was added to the list of birds that can be legally killed as a 'pest species' without the need for a licence.

Meanwhile another species of parrot, the monk parakeet from South America, is now being culled. This is partly because the species builds huge nests out of sticks (the only one of the world's 370 or so species of parrot to do so), which could threaten the electricity grid if built on pylons; and partly because the current population of around 100 to 150 birds (mainly in the Borehamwood area just north of London) is small enough to be easily eradicated. But killing tens of thousands of ring-necked parakeets, most of which live in parks and gardens, would be a very difficult, if not impossible, task.

That's partly because Londoners have mostly taken this exotic bird to their hearts, especially when parakeets visit their gardens, perching awkwardly on seed and peanut feeders while removing the contents with that highly effective beak. But not everyone is so enamoured with these noisy birds: the Urban Birder David Lindo, who sees parakeets regularly on his local patch at Wormwood Scrubs in north-west London, has called for them to be eradicated.

Once, when giving a talk at the eponymous prison, he told his audience that the parakeets should be sent back to where they came from. One prisoner, a bulky white gentleman, pointed his chubby finger at David (whose parents came here from Jamaica in the late 1950s) and announced, 'You know what you are, mate? You're a f***ing racist, you are!'

This exchange encapsulates the complex issues we face when dealing with introduced species; indeed, even the vocabulary we use – words such as 'alien', 'invasive' and 'foreign' – have led some to accuse those calling for a cull of being in favour of some form of ethnic cleansing. The truth is of course far more complex than this, and drawing analogies between the arrival of human immigrants, and plants and animals that have colonised the UK, is not particularly helpful or enlightening.

What we do know is that the ring-necked parakeet is just one of dozens, perhaps hundreds, of species from abroad that have managed to make their home in our towns and cities. Some thrive and spread, as we have already seen in the case of the grey squirrel and muntjac, thereby causing problems for our native wildlife. Others, such as the little owl, seem to be more benevolent, and we welcome them.

The flocks of ring-necked parakeets shooting across the London skyline on a summer's evening, their calls echoing in the air as they disappear, are at the centre of this complex argument. They might, it is true, cause damage both to other bird species and to our agricultural industry. On the other hand, it cannot be denied that they add a splash of colour and excitement to our capital's wildlife. So perhaps, for the time being at least, we should give them the benefit of the doubt.

❀

THE ABILITY OF wild creatures to either move from their original rural habitats into new, urban ones, or to colonise what is for them a totally new and alien environment, is little short of miraculous. Yet our city wildlife still needs all the help it can get, for not every species can find an analogue habitat to replace their wild one. Some still need us to create new, purpose-built refuges where they can live and thrive.

Almost forty years ago, as a teenage birder living on the fringes of West London, I stumbled across Barn Elms Reservoirs. Lying on the south bank of the Thames, by the huge bend in the river between Putney and Hammersmith where the Oxford and Cambridge Boat Race runs its annual course, these four stark, concrete basins surrounded by short-cropped grass did not at first sight appear to be much of a hotspot for birds.

But having climbed over the fence to get in (you were supposed to obtain an official permit in advance, but I never had the foresight to do so), I was astonished at what I found. In winter, especially when cold weather to the north and east forced waterbirds to find alternative places to feed, Barn Elms was thronged with ducks, geese and swans.

It was here that I got my best-ever views of goosanders, a colourful diving duck memorably described by TV presenter Kate Humble as looking like a cormorant in drag. Many years later, I stopped off on my way back from work to watch a white-winged black tern, a rare visitor from Continental Europe, floating over the waters to feed. By that time, just before the turn of the millennium, the reservoirs were in the process of being converted into what would become one of the best-known urban nature reserves in the world. This transformation was the vision of one man: the twentieth century's best-known bird artist and conservationist, Sir Peter Scott.

Before he died in 1989, Peter Scott completed one final painting to add to his extraordinary lifetime's work. It showed the view from the south-western corner of Barn Elms towards the River Thames, but not a view that anyone had ever seen. It was a vision of what the place might look like if it were transformed into an urban nature reserve.

Clouds of wigeon and shoveler hang in the air, forever coming in to land; while beneath, areas of open water surrounded by reed beds are thronged with even more birds. The picture could be depicting a scene from one of our great wild wetlands – the Ouse Washes, perhaps, or the Somerset Levels – were it not for the distant silhouettes of tower blocks studded along the far horizon. For this is a remarkably accurate portrait of a place Scott never lived to see completed: the London Wetland Centre.

When they were no longer needed, Barn Elms Reservoirs could have been concreted over and turned into just another housing estate. But Scott and his successors at the Wildfowl and Wetlands Trust hatched a clever plan, selling off a small proportion of the area for luxury homes, which funded the conversion of the vast majority of the site – more than 100 acres in total – to a refuge for urban wildlife.

The London Wetland Centre is now a haven for all kinds of wild creatures, and well over 200 species of bird have been recorded here, including avocets, bitterns and migrant ospreys. It is also, of course, a haven for people: more than a quarter of a million city dwellers visit the site each year, enjoying a breath of country air amidst these urban surroundings, just 4 miles from Buckingham Palace.

Today, as I head along the bleached wooden boardwalk into the reserve, with lemon-yellow brimstone butterflies dancing alongside me, and jewel-like hawker dragonflies buzzing back and forth in search of prey, it's hard for me to remember what this place was like in its old industrial incarnation. I reach the top of a sunny bank on the western boundary of the reserve, where I have been told there is a chance of finding something special. Carefully lifting a piece of corrugated iron, I discover what I am looking for: a writhing coil of sleek bronzed bodies. Not sunbathers, but slow worms.

Elsewhere on the reserve, lapwings tumble in the air above their nests, calling constantly to deter the menacing crows that threaten their eggs and chicks at every moment of the day. Another bird you might not expect to see – the common tern – also breeds here, nesting on artificial islands covered with netting to deter predators. And from deep inside a rough area of scrub on the edge of the lagoon comes an unmistakable sound: the ridiculously loud outburst of song that can only come from one bird, the elusive Cetti's warbler.

Because it only colonised Britain from Continental Europe in the past few decades, this is a species I never dreamed of hearing here when I first visited the site back in the 1970s. But one bird I would have seen – and indeed, which could be found almost everywhere in London in those days – has now vanished not just from here but also from many of its former haunts: the house sparrow.

❀

IN CASE WE assume that our city wildlife is doing just fine, or are seduced by the litany of good-news stories about colonists such as the peregrine, the tale of two familiar creatures – the house sparrow and the hedgehog – should give us pause for thought.

The once-widespread sparrow – so common here that it became synonymous with the capital itself, as the 'cockney sparrer' – has now vanished from not just much of London, but from many British cities. Its tuneless but friendly chirping was once the soundtrack to our urban lives, yet today the sparrows have fallen silent.

About the time that I was breaking and entering into Barn Elms Reservoirs, I would also enjoy more wholesome encounters with birds. My mother and I would take the train up to Waterloo and cross over the river into St James's Park, where a kindly old man used to feed the sparrows. If I shyly approached him he would pour some birdseed into my palm, telling me to hold it out for the birds. Within seconds, my hand would be covered with sparrows, eagerly wolfing down the free meal.

He became something of a tourist attraction, with passing Japanese and American visitors snapping happily away with their Kodaks. But today he wouldn't be there at all, because there are no sparrows for him, or indeed anyone else, to feed. Bearing in mind that in 1925 the young ornithologist Max Nicholson counted more than 2,500 sparrows in nearby Kensington Gardens (where there are now none), this is a truly unprecedented decline.

Today, one of the very few places in central London where you can more or less guarantee seeing sparrows is, ironically, London Zoo. Thanks to the presence of large captive animals, their food and the insects they attract, a small colony of sparrows still breeds here. Some have, bizarrely, turned carnivorous; I once watched them enter the vultures' cage at feeding time to consume morsels of raw red meat.

Why the sparrow has declined so dramatically and so rapidly is still largely a mystery. We know that numbers have fallen in the countryside because of a lack of seeds left on stubble fields in autumn and winter, as a result of the year-round cultivation of arable crops such as wheat.

We also know that the tidier and more upmarket an area becomes, the fewer the sparrows that live there – for they like messy corners in both cities and the countryside, where they can find plenty of places to build their nests. Certainly, around my Somerset home, an eighteenth-century farmhouse surrounded by farmyards, hedgerows and plenty of livestock, sparrows are still thriving.

But this still doesn't explain why sparrows have disappeared from the hearts of our cities. One unproven but highly plausible theory is that being so sedentary in their habits – city sparrows rarely venture more than a mile from where they were born – these little birds are disproportionately affected by toxic chemicals produced by vehicle exhausts, especially those from diesel engines. This idea gains credence because it was put forward by the world's expert on sparrows, the nonagenarian J. Denis Summers-Smith. He is not only a highly skilled ornithologist with more than seventy years spent studying sparrows under his belt, but he was also, in his professional career, an industrial chemist.

Another reason may lie in the house sparrow's complex family life. Sparrows are – rather like us – highly sociable beings, nesting in colonies where their noisy chatter seems to stimulate them to raise a family. Perhaps as numbers drop below a critical level, the sparrows somehow lose the will to breed, and so rapidly disappear.

It is certainly true that you rarely see a single sparrow: they are either present in reasonable numbers, or not at all. But whatever the cause of its decline, the fact remains that in Britain, more house sparrows have disappeared than any other species. More than 20 million of these cheeky little birds have vanished since Bobby Moore lifted the World Cup just down the road from London Zoo, at Wembley in 1966.

❁

WHEREAS HOUSE SPARROWS have lived alongside human beings for many centuries, another once-common creature was originally a country dweller. But as its rural habitats began to fragment and disappear, so it sought refuge in our urban areas.

As its name suggests, the hedgehog is closely associated with the hedgerows that form borders between farmed fields and other rural habitats throughout lowland Britain. Hedgerows have been rapidly disappearing since the end of the Second World War, as the result of that misguided agricultural revolution whose primary aim was to maximise the amount of food grown in our countryside, at whatever cost to the wider environment. This has led, as we've seen, to a wholesale destruction of semi-natural habitats formed over hundreds, sometimes thousands, of years.

Hedgerows have been among the biggest casualties, with an estimated 480,000 kilometres (300,000 miles) lost since 1945 – more than the distance between the earth and the moon. Even in more recent, supposedly enlightened times, the losses have continued: one estimate suggests that 80,000 kilometres (50,000 miles) of hedgerows were lost in just five years in the late 1980s.

It's not just the loss of hedgerows that has led to hedgehogs' demise. They have also suffered from the destruction of woodlands, from the use of agricultural chemicals that not only kill the insects on which they depend but also poison them directly, and especially from the rise in traffic on our roads. Hardly surprising, then, that Britain's hedgehog population has declined by as much as 97 per cent, from 30 million animals in 1950 to fewer than 1 million today.

To try to escape the problems in the countryside, many hedgehogs have found a refuge in towns and cities, especially in our gardens. But even here they are not safe: the widespread use of slug pellets, now thankfully in decline, has wreaked havoc with our urban hedgehog population, as has the fad for covering lawns and flower beds with wooden decking, and especially the habit of fencing off our gardens from those of our neighbours.

Hedgehogs are wandering souls, and in spring the males travel several miles in a single night in search of receptive females with which they can mate. For this they need, ideally, a permeable network of gardens, with holes and gaps in fences and walls so they can move easily between one garden and the next. Faced with the barriers we often erect between our back yards and those of our neighbours, hedgehogs often have no choice but to venture out onto city streets, where many thousands of them are run over as they try to cross busy roads.

One imaginative solution to try to reverse the urban hedgehog's decline is a simple but effective initiative known as 'Hedgehog Street'. More than 35,000 people up and down the country have already signed up to the scheme, and discovered how they and their neighbours can make their own street hedgehog friendly. They do so by removing barriers, providing the right kind of food (cat food rather than the bread and milk we used to feed these little beasts, which gives them indigestion), and encouraging people to report hedgehog sightings so that we know where they are thriving.

Schemes like this are a great way to get people involved in saving one of our favourite wild animals, and also to create the kind of community spirit that will lead to people understanding the wider value of wildlife and nature, especially in an urban context. But for the hedgehog, this may be too little, too late – this creature of the countryside may simply not be able to adapt quickly enough to cope with modern city life.

❋

BOTH HEDGEHOGS AND house sparrows can still be found in one very familiar, and until relatively recently overlooked, habitat: urban gardens. With a total area of at least 1 million acres – bigger than the entire county of

Suffolk – Britain's gardens collectively make up an area described by wildlife gardening guru Chris Baines as 'Britain's biggest nature reserve'.

But until the second half of the twentieth century, the importance of gardens for wildlife was virtually ignored. The term 'garden birds' was not even coined until the end of the Second World War, in a modest little book written by the secretary of the RSPB, Phyllis Barclay-Smith. And for much of the post-war era, the only food we provided for avian visitors to our gardens was a few scraps of leftovers or stale bread. Even as late as the 1970s, the only bird food widely available was small boxes of seeds marketed as Swoop, and mainly sold in pet shops.

'Wildlife gardening' was not a concept any naturalist – or indeed gardener – would recognise. When Chris Baines first created a wildlife garden at the Chelsea Flower Show, in 1985 – when most gardeners regarded wild flowers as 'weeds' – his winner's medal was mistakenly inscribed, 'Chris Baines, for a wildfire [*sic*] garden'.

Today, just thirty or so years later, things could hardly be more different. Gardening for wildlife has entered the mainstream, and according to the RSPB, two out of three households in Britain feed their garden birds. Given that 80 per cent of us live in urban areas, the majority of these gardens are in towns and cities.

We spend more than £150 million a year in doing so; a drop in the ocean, admittedly, compared with the £15 billion we spend on our pets, but a significant sum nevertheless. Designer foods such as kibbled sunflower hearts and nyger seed (preferred by every self-respecting goldfinch) have now displaced common-or-garden peanuts; while the array of different feeders on offer in garden centres looks like nature's equivalent of the Ideal Home Exhibition. Even the Royal Family have got in on the act: in late 2014 the nation's favourite gardener, Alan Titchmarsh, presented a series of television programmes on prime-time ITV featuring Buckingham Palace Garden, and noting its status as a haven for wildlife in the middle of London.

We feed garden birds partly because we want to help them – and there is plenty of evidence that smaller species, such as the long-tailed tit and goldfinch, which might otherwise perish in hard winters, survive thanks to our generosity. But we also do it for more selfish reasons, because seeing 'our' birds on a daily basis brings us pleasure and delight. As Sir David Attenborough noted on the BBC4 series 'Birds Britannia':

[Garden birds] bring a breath of the natural world, the non-human world, and they're the one thing that does. They're also magical, in that they suddenly take off and disappear and you've no idea where they've gone – yet they come back again.

Birder and TV presenter Bill Oddie, whose own north London garden is awash with bird feeders and nest boxes – as well as garden gnomes – believes that for many people, especially those living in towns and cities:

> There is nothing but garden birds – the only birds they actually see are in their garden!

Many of the more than half a million people who take part in the RSPB's Big Garden Birdwatch each January would probably endorse his view.

Of course, the term 'garden birds' is just as much of an artificial construct as are the bird tables and feeding stations we provide for their benefit. Many of the species found in our gardens are those that evolved in ancient woodlands, while others are normally found on the woodland edge, in hedgerows or on traditional farmland.

The long-term degradation and destruction of these habitats has, over the years since the Second World War, forced these species to venture into our towns and cities and form a mutually beneficial relationship with us. They take our food, they drink and bathe in our water, and they nest in the homes we provide, while we enjoy watching them. Thus robins and blue tits, blackbirds and song thrushes, and many more, have transformed from shy and unfamiliar woodland species to now being some of our most familiar – and favourite – birds.

But these birds didn't simply swap one habitat for a less productive substitute. It turns out that gardens are not simply small patches of substandard countryside; they are in fact considerably better places for birds than those we think of as natural habitats, such as woods and farmland. Today, blackbirds and song thrushes breed at densities up to ten times greater in gardens than in their original woodland home; blue and great tits find plenty of opportunities to nest in artificial nest boxes; and all our garden birds enjoy the avian equivalent of a five-star hotel and restaurant, on tap, every single day of the year.

It's not just birds. Badgers and bats, foxes and frogs, grass snakes and slow worms, and many more creatures, have all benefited from the way our gardens provide a network of mini-habitats, with food, water and plenty of places to hide, sleep and breed. Insects benefit because unlike the farmed countryside, gardens are (mostly) pesticide-free, enabling bumblebees and hoverflies, butterflies and moths, and a host of other invertebrates, to thrive.

Much of the evidence for the importance of gardens for wildlife comes from a single groundbreaking study. For more than thirty years an urban ecologist, Jennifer Owen, studied the wildlife of her own suburban garden in the city of Leicester. During this time, she discovered a mind-boggling total of 2,673 different species: including 474 plants, 54 birds, and an incredible 1,997 different kinds of insects.

Yet this is just the tip of a remarkably large iceberg: Owen estimates that if the more difficult invertebrate groups were studied in the same detail, her garden might play host to as many as 8,000 different species. And lest you imagine that this is a particularly special garden, it is not: Owen herself believes that most urban and suburban gardens support an equally wide range of wildlife.

What cannot be in doubt is that, given the way the wider countryside has become so unfriendly towards wildlife, Britain's gardens provide a crucial and continuing lifeline, a vital and welcome oasis in a hostile land. But while gardens are undoubtedly good for wildlife, we mustn't forget that garden wildlife is equally good for us. At a time when we are beginning to realise the importance of the natural world in our lives, there are few better ways to get a regular dose of nature than by creating a wildlife-friendly garden.

More studies are needed to measure the importance of garden birds and wildlife to our mental and spiritual health and well-being. But anyone who has spent any length of time enjoying the complex and fascinating behaviour of birds in their garden knows that doing so is good for the soul.

❋

NOT EVERY CITY dweller owns, or has access to, a garden. For them, those other little patches of green – parks and playing fields, urban commons and areas of waste ground – are ever more valuable, because they provide a unique opportunity to engage with nature on a regular basis. For, as has now been confirmed beyond doubt, nature is good for us. But for it to really have an effect it cannot just be a bolt-on extra, to be experienced only when we venture out into the 'countryside'. Instead, it needs to be available on people's doorsteps.

Early one May morning, I visit one such place, getting my daily fix of nature in a very different setting from that of my rural home, though one that is strangely reminiscent, in both sights and sounds, of a typically rural idyll.

As the sun filters through the trees, the dawn chorus is already in full swing, with the fluting baritones of the blackbirds and song thrushes underpinning the tenor songs of the blackcaps and robins. Low in the canopy, a chiffchaff calls its name, insistently and persistently, until you might think it would get tired of doing so; while in the blossomy branches above, a great tit utters a syncopated version of the same two syllables, 'tea-*cher*, tea-*cher*, tea-*cher* . . .' over and over again.

On the woodland floor below, cowslips and bluebells form a patchwork carpet, hemmed in by wild garlic, whose powerful odour fills the air. A fox picks his way carefully through the foliage, stopping momentarily to glance at me before walking on. A grey squirrel shins up a nearby tree where, in the very topmost twigs, a gaudy ring-necked parakeet the colour of a lime-green ice lolly serenades the rising sun in his own, uniquely raucous fashion.

Apart, perhaps, from the presence of the parakeet, and the blocks of flats just visible through the trees, I can almost imagine that I am in the middle of the countryside. And yet this place is the very heart of our capital, barely 2 miles from the City of London, and just off the busy, bustling Mile End Road. Welcome to Tower Hamlets Cemetery Park.

This is the real urban jungle: the nearest ancient woodland to London's city centre, and a much-needed oasis both for wildlife and people. And as dawn gives way to early morning, they begin to appear. Cyclists: of both the recreational and commuting varieties, some clad top-to-toe in Lycra, others in business suits, briefcases strapped to their bike-racks. Schoolchildren: the younger ones accompanied by their parents, with smaller siblings in buggies; the older ones on their own, or in little gaggles of three or four, joshing one another and letting off steam before they have to settle down in silence for the first lesson of the day.

As well as the trees and shrubs, bushes and hedgerows, wild flowers and songbirds, the Cemetery Park is – as you might expect – chock-full of tumbledown stone monuments, shrines and statues. Each grave is marked with a dilapidated grey headstone, stained with lichens and topped with moss, a timely warning that we have a limited span on this earth, so that time spent with nature is never wasted. But the presence of so many dead is not unsettling, as you might expect; it is somehow comforting.

Being here is like pressing the pause button in our busy lives: a refuge from deadlines and emails, smartphones and text messages, computers and TV, where there's never any time to just sit still, to wait and watch, and simply take in what nature has to offer. So as I sit on a flat, worn gravestone, watching a blackbird balancing on another, and listen to the chorus of birdsong, I can begin to appreciate just how valuable this place is for those lucky enough to live close by.

And yet it could all have been so different. Tower Hamlets Cemetery was not originally created as a recreational facility; but out of simple, practical need. Until the Victorian era, London's dead were buried in small, local churchyards, just as they still are in more rural, less populous parts of Britain.

But with the coming of the Industrial Revolution, London's population almost doubled, from about 750,000 people in 1760 to nearly 1.5 million by 1815, making this the largest city in the world. This sudden surge in numbers was creating huge problems for small urban graveyards, increasing the risk of disease and contamination of the water supply.

Something had to be done, and in true Victorian spirit, it was: in less than a decade, from 1832 to 1841, seven large public cemeteries – known to posterity as the 'Magnificent Seven' – were created around the fringes of London. The last of these to be opened was Tower Hamlets. In its first half-century alone, almost 250,000 bodies were interred here, the vast majority in unmarked, public graves, because their families could not afford to buy an individual plot. Although the cemetery continued to be open to new burials until the 1960s, it finally closed in 1966 when the trend towards cremations meant that there was less demand for traditional funerals.

This presented the local authority with a problem – what should they do with the place? Plans were made to clear all the gravestones, and turn it into a typical urban park, with neat, short-cropped lawns, swings and slides and a football pitch or two; but soon after the grave clearances began, local people objected, and the work was stopped. The site was then almost sold for development, but again, people fought a campaign to stop this going ahead, and eventually won. Finally, more than thirty years after the cemetery had closed for burials, it was reopened – this time as a local nature reserve.

The cemetery park is managed by Ken Greenway, a local lad in his early thirties, whose sheer passion for being here is evident the moment you meet him. Ken took the job as a young graduate ten years ago, expecting to stay for a year or two before moving on, but so fell in love with the place that he has made it his own. For the past decade he and the Friends of Tower Hamlets Cemetery Park have encouraged both wildlife and people – and it's worked. Yet how easily things could have gone in a very different direction, with the land lost for ever to the developers.

❀

IN THE SCHEME of things, it could perhaps be argued that if Britain's urban wildlife habitats were to vanish overnight, we would have lost very little. Apart from a handful of specialised species such as the black redstart, very few creatures depend on urban habitats – they can almost all be found somewhere else in the country.

But this would be to miss the point. The reason why urban wildlife is so crucial to our existence is, as my visit to Tower Hamlets proved, because of its beneficial effect on us. Those sites saved from development are valuable not just because they support a wide range of plants and animals, but also because they provide a place where local people can visit and engage with nature in an urban setting.

For more than four out of five Britons – well over fifty million people and rising – living and working in our towns and cities, urban wildlife is the only nature they are ever likely to encounter in their busy, frantic and ever more pressurised lives.

Ironically, perhaps, I only really began to appreciate this after moving from London to the Somerset countryside, almost a decade ago. Looking back, I realise that for many years in my twenties and thirties – when I was forging a career and bringing up a young family – I hardly had any engagement with nature at all. Living in Finsbury Park and working at White City – two of the most urbanised areas of the capital – I would only realise that spring had come when I heard the first swifts screaming across the skies in the first week of May.

But living in the city did teach me one important thing: that what matters most is not the rare, but the commonplace. And what also matters is simply engaging with the natural world; finding the time to step outside our daily lives for an hour or so, and enter a world we cannot control, and which is constantly able to surprise. Whether we live in the heart of a city or the remotest corner of our countryside, we all need wildlife to sustain and enrich our lives. For if we lose touch with nature, we will eventually lose touch with who we are.

7

The Accidental Countryside

Other Artificial Habitats

It is a happy event if a rare bird nests in a Norfolk
sea-marsh, in a Scottish forest, on a Welsh mountain.
If it nests on the outskirts of a large city, in the
messy limbo that is neither town nor country, where
suburban buildings, factories, petrol stations and
trunk roads sprawl and blight, the event takes on an
extra piquancy.

Kenneth Allsop, *Adventure Lit Their Star* (1949)

FEWER PEOPLE HAVE stood where I am now than have
reached the summit of Mount Everest. Yet just out of
sight, beyond the trees, the distant hum of traffic reminds
me that more than 100,000 people pass by this spot every
single day.

I'm just 25 miles north-west of the centre of London, on
a small triangle of land in the middle of the junction
between two of the busiest motorways in Britain, the M25
and the M40. When the M25 was built, back in the 1980s,
the planners somehow overlooked this little patch – about
40 acres in all – leaving behind a hidden haven for wildlife.

Nobody, apart from the odd highway engineer, ever visits here.

As dawn breaks on a May morning, I have the place all to myself. From deep inside a dense stand of sallows, a blackcap sings his soft, tuneful warble, almost immediately answered by the higher pitched trill of a wren. I can hear a song thrush delivering his message over and over again, emphasising his claim to his territory. And beyond, the deeper, flutier notes of a blackbird, along with the laughing call of a green woodpecker as it bounds away into the distance.

Despite the lateness of this particular spring, the trees, shrubs and bushes are now in full flow, with clumps of white hawthorn blossom studding the greenery, and custard-yellow clusters of gorse adding a welcome splash of colour. Frogs poke their heads momentarily above the surface of a small pond, before sinking back out of sight.

Bumblebees buzz from flower to flower, their furry legs covered with pollen. And all around me, a selection of spring butterflies – with comma, small tortoiseshell and the Jaffa-winged orange-tip among them – settle with their wings open to soak up the early-morning sunshine. I feel a sense of peace and quiet, of being alone in an overcrowded world.

❁

BRITAIN IS FULL of little fragments of land like this: scraps, corners and patches, abandoned, derelict and mostly forgotten. Yet these places, scattered up and down the country, add up to an area far bigger than all our official nature reserves put together. We are inclined to dismiss them as 'wasteland', and yet as Richard Mabey pointed out more than forty years ago in his book *The Unofficial Countryside*, they provide refuges where 'birds, mammals and insects flourish against the odds in the most obscure and surprising places'.

Not that these places are easy to define. Some are ancient; others were created only a year or two ago. Some are in the middle of urban areas, others in the heart of the countryside. Many are in suburbia – memorably defined by author and broadcaster Kenneth Allsop as 'the messy limbo that is neither town nor country'.

They exist on the edges of our lives: indeed, poets Michael Symmons Roberts and Paul Farley have dubbed them 'edgelands'. The subtitle to their book of that name is 'Journeys into England's True Wilderness', a claim that might at first seem absurd, but the more we explore these forgotten places, the more accurate it appears. Because many of these sites are no longer useful to us, the wildlife has been able move back in. At a time when our 'official' countryside is under more and more pressure to produce cheap food, or being covered with concrete to build roads, factories and houses, they are a crucial lifeline, keeping some declining species afloat.

What also strikes me is just how varied they are. Some were created centuries, even millennia ago: ancient monuments whose structures now provide a home for some of our scarcest creatures, from sand lizards to stoats and natterjack toads to orchids. Others are by-products of our long industrial heritage: among them disused factories, quarries and gravel pits; while some are part of the infrastructure of our transport network, such as railway cuttings, roadside verges and canal banks.

There are military sites: vast tracts of land closed off from public access, where wild creatures can get on with their lives without being disturbed – apart, of course, from the odd exploding shell. But there are also very public places, such as golf courses and theme parks, created to meet our modern craving for sports and leisure activities.

All these places may appear very different from one another, yet they have one crucial thing in common: none of them were originally created as a home for wildlife. Instead, we designed and made them for our own needs and requirements. But in doing so, we took them out of the farmed countryside, thus inadvertently preventing them from being sprayed, mown and generally 'improved' – an agricultural euphemism which for wildlife, ironically, means the very opposite of what it implies. So without ever meaning to, we have created a huge chain of accidental nature reserves: unplanned and unintended, yet vital for the survival of all sorts of wild creatures.

The downside is that because we often don't recognise these places' value to nature, they can be very vulnerable, and are easily destroyed. But there's an upside too: for these hidden, secret corners of the British countryside can provide us with some of the most unexpected and memorable wildlife encounters imaginable. It may seem counter-intuitive, but these odd little pieces of land, scattered up and down the country in the most unlikely places, offer one of our best hopes for making room for wildlife.

❀

OUR ANCESTORS WEREN'T particularly concerned with the welfare of Britain's wild creatures; the saving of human souls was far more central to their lives. And so from the time that Saint Augustine came to these islands on a mission to convert the heathen Britons to Christianity, almost 1,500 years ago, they built churches – many of which, having been demolished, rebuilt and extended over the centuries, still survive today.

That continuity hasn't only been central to human lives; it has helped our wildlife too. For many plants and animals, the key factor in their continued survival is stability: finding a place to live that doesn't change very much over time. All over Britain, there's one quiet corner of every parish that provides exactly that: churchyards.

For most of us, whether we are religious or not, churchyards are places of peace, quiet and contemplation. Largely unaltered over time, they provide an island of stability and continuity in a rapidly changing world: an undisturbed corner of the countryside where wild creatures can find a home.

In my own parish church of St Mark in Somerset, as in churchyards up and down the country, jackdaws call out their name from the summit of the tall stone tower, while blackbirds and song thrushes forage for crimson berries in the evergreen foliage of an ancient yew tree, just outside the church door. Wood mice feed on seeds and nuts amongst the gravestones, while a robin perches jauntily on top of another ancient monument, the original inscription long since worn away by centuries of wind and rain.

Hidden away inside the tower itself, a colony of pipistrelle bats has found a home – where else, but inside the belfry? They emerge at dusk in a flurry of wings, their calls too high-pitched for us to perceive, but detectable with the aid of a neat little gadget: my bat detector, which converts the bats' calls into loud clicks which I can then hear. As dusk falls, I hear the distant hoot of a tawny owl: the sound of the male, immediately answered with the piercing 'kee-wick' call of the female, one of the few duets among British birds. I imagine the wood mouse cowering in fear, before scuttling rapidly away into the darkness.

The most extraordinary form of life here is one that most people overlook. Yet paradoxically, it is all around us: on the gravestones, the trunks and branches of the trees, and covering the walls of the church itself. These mysterious organisms are neither entirely plants nor animals, but lichens.

Lichens are a peculiar life form: a symbiotic relationship between two different organisms that work together for mutual benefit. They are made up of a fungus, which provides the majority of the organism we see, and an alga, which enables the lichen to photosynthesise and thus obtain the energy it needs to grow and survive.

Lichens have some remarkable qualities. They are amongst the oldest organisms in the natural world; some of those covering the ancient gravestones in my local churchyard may have been growing since Tudor times, while the oldest colonies have been dated back 9,000 years, to the time when woolly mammoths were still roaming the land. They are very varied – there are more than 1,700 different species in Britain alone – and also incredibly tough; able to cope with whatever the elements throw at them, from wind and rain to sun, sleet and snow.

As winter frosts take their grip on the surface of the stones, the lichen shuts down its operating system and simply waits for the thaw to come. In summer droughts, as the surface temperature rises to desert-like conditions, lichens are able to survive without drying out and dying. And as soon as the rain begins to fall again, they burst into life once more.

Yet lichens do face one major problem: they are incredibly sensitive to pollution. The Industrial Revolution brought profit and social change to Britain, but disaster for our lichens. Smoke and soot filled the air, and in the industrial heartlands of Yorkshire and Lancashire, and great cities such as London, they began to die. There was one place they could find a welcome sanctuary: rural churchyards like this one. And now that our air is again clean and fit to breathe, lichens are thriving, and recolonising our towns and cities once more.

❁

THE INDUSTRIAL REVOLUTION may have been a temporary setback for Britain's lichens, but for other plants and animals it provided a new opportunity to spread throughout the country – thanks to Britain's growing transport system. From the middle of the nineteenth century until well into the twentieth, railways, canals and roads created new networks: artificial corridors by which plants and animals could spread throughout the country. The story of one once-obscure and foreign plant sums up their success at doing so.

Today, the Oxford ragwort's raggedy stems topped with vibrant yellow flowers are a familiar summer sight throughout much of Britain. Yet just over three centuries ago this plant was found no nearer to here than central and south-eastern Europe, where it flourished on rocky mountainsides, including the arid slopes of Mount Etna in Sicily.

The plant was first brought to Britain around the year 1700, and was later planted in the Oxford Botanic

Garden in the centre of that city. It survived there virtually unremarked for almost a century, before being noticed growing 'in the wild' on the walls outside the garden in 1794. In the century or so since it first arrived in the botanic garden, it managed to spread only a mile or two away. It might have remained rare and localised for ever, as a mere footnote in the history of botany, were it not for the coming of the railways.

On 12 June 1844, the Great Western Railway finally reached Oxford, and the fortunes of this humble ragwort began to change. Like many wild flowers, the Oxford ragwort spreads its seeds by attaching them to little parachutes of hairs, which enable them to float away on a gust of wind. And the trains running up and down the line to Oxford provided exactly what it needed. As the botanist George Claridge Druce wrote in his *Flora of Oxfordshire*, published in 1927:

> The vortex of air following the express carries the fruits [*sic*] in its wake. I have seen the seeds enter a railway-carriage window near Oxford and remain suspended in the air of the compartment until they found an exit near Tilehurst.

It wasn't just the movement of the trains, carrying the seeds along in their slipstream, which enabled the ragwort to spread so rapidly. The clinker along the tracks – small stones creating a stable, well-drained bed on which the rails could run efficiently – created an ideal habitat, almost exactly mimicking the arid slopes of its native Mount Etna. Few native plants can survive in such a hostile environment, so in the absence of competition, the newcomer thrived.

By 1899, the Oxford ragwort had reached Devon and Warwickshire, and by 1916 it could be found in north Wales. Then it received another boost to its fortunes, as botanical historian Geoffrey Grigson pointed out in his classic work *An Englishman's Flora*:

> Two things occurred to make the Oxford ragwort's fortune – first the railways were built, then the bombs were dropped.

The devastation of the Second World War created newly opened ground on bomb sites, many of which remained open and undeveloped well into the 1950s. Just like the railways, these provided the ideal rubble-strewn habitat for this adaptable plant, and the spread of the Oxford ragwort continued apace. It thrived alongside another familiar plant of waste ground, the rosebay willowherb, whose bright pinkish-mauve flowers bring a splash of colour to road verges and railway cuttings throughout the summer months.

Today both plants can be found on areas of rough ground throughout much of Britain, though the ragwort remains scarce in Scotland and northern England, and is more restricted to our towns and cities than its fellow traveller – which, given that like other ragworts it is toxic to livestock, is a small blessing. As an unexpected bonus, the spread of Oxford ragwort also boosted the fortunes of the cinnabar moth, whose tiger-striped caterpillars feed on its leaves.

❀

LIKE THE RAILWAYS, our road network has provided another of these hidden habitats. Britain's network of motorways and major roads stretches for 6,000 miles, about the same distance as from London to Tokyo. On either side of these, what is effectively a vast linear nature reserve criss-crosses the country, with a combined area bigger than Dartmoor.

Roadside verges are crucial havens for wildlife for two reasons. First, because they are not ploughed or planted with crops, unlike the farmland beyond; and second, because they provide corridors along which plants and animals can travel. So although this doesn't make up for the massive destruction our road network has wrought on the British countryside, it does at least provide a compensatory home for some of our wild creatures.

As I drive along the M4 between London and the West Country, I often see a familiar silhouette hovering above the verges. The kestrel is sometimes called the 'motorway hawk' because of its habit of hunting over the edges of the carriageways, and although this slender falcon is not as common as it used to be, it can still be seen searching intently for voles along many of our motorways and trunk roads.

Roadside verges are havens for voles and mice because the grass is rarely mown or sprayed with chemicals, meaning that there are plenty of seeds, nuts and insects on which these tiny animals feed. One species, the field vole, has thrived in these new habitats; with almost 80 million individuals, it is the only British wild mammal to outnumber the human inhabitants of these islands. And many other species – including the kestrel – take advantage of its abundance, using their ability to see ultraviolet wavelengths to detect the urine trails made by the voles.

However, even with the increase in the road network since the 1970s, kestrel numbers have fallen by almost half during the same period, and the species has now gone from having once been the commonest raptor in Britain to third place, behind the buzzard and sparrowhawk. Why this should have happened, at a time when every other British raptor species is either stable or increasing, is a bit of a puzzle, though our old enemy agricultural intensification is at least partly to blame. Another, perhaps even more serious problem, is the increased use of powerful rodenticides, chemical poisons that kill another species that depends on voles, and which also hunts along roadside verges, the barn owl. The kestrel is a salutary warning: edgelands may be good for wildlife, but they may not be enough to save some species from decline.

❁

LATTERLY, ANOTHER RAPTOR has joined the kestrel to hunt for small mammals along our motorway verges. The red kite is now a familiar sight along many of our major roads, with flocks of several dozen birds regularly seen above the M40 between London and Oxford, while friends of mine in the centre of Reading often see them floating over their back garden. They are also commonly seen in Scotland's Black Isle and the border country of Dumfries and Galloway, in England's East Midlands, and of course in their original stronghold, mid-Wales.

Yet little more than a century ago the red kite was on the verge of disappearing as a British breeding bird, with just a handful of individuals left, including a single breeding female, confined to the hidden valleys of mid-Wales. Like any bird sporting a hooked beak and sharp talons, the kite had become the target of farmers and gamekeepers, and by the mid-nineteenth century anyone who owned the newly invented breech-loading shotgun, and could accurately aim and fire it.

We may have driven the kite to the verge of extinction; but we also brought it back. In the late 1980s, young kites were flown here from Spain, then tagged and released in the Chiltern Hills to the north-west of London. I can still remember my surprise at hearing the news: surely this scarce bird of prey would need truly wild places in order to live; not the mixture of farmland, woodland, villages, towns and roads squeezed into a crowded, bustling corner of the Home Counties.

Then I remembered that kites have form when it comes to living alongside people. Long before they were persecuted, they were valued as the clean-up squad of Elizabethan London: scavenging for any waste products they could eat, and so helping to keep the streets cleaner than they would have been without these adaptable and opportunistic birds.

So you might think that the newly released kites would be welcomed with open arms. Yet to their shame, many people who should have known better were vehemently opposed to the reintroduction of the red kite to Britain. A few old-fashioned conservationists moaned about 'interfering with nature', while even some birdwatchers complained that these would not be 'real kites' – as if a bird becoming common would somehow devalue its rarity. More predictably, some farmers and gamekeepers formed alliances to try to prevent the kites being released.

Even when the reintroduction had begun, persecution, while far less widespread than it used to be, was still a major threat to the birds' success. This was especially true in Scotland, where the reintroduced populations in Dumfries and Galloway and on the Black Isle are still being routinely poisoned, trapped and shot – all, of course, illegally. This is despite the fact that kites are a significant contributor to the growing industry of 'wildlife tourism', with many people visiting these locations specifically to see and enjoy the kites.

Two places have embraced the kite more than most: one is the original home of these birds, in mid-Wales, the other the newest release site, in north-east England. Here, red kites have been released back into a true 'edgeland': along the Derwent Valley, which runs south-west from the town of Gateshead into rural Tyne and Wear. The Northern Kites project began in 2004, and during the following three years almost 100 red kites were released here.

On a windswept March afternoon I am standing with the project's manager Keith Bowey on the edge of a housing estate, on the western outskirts of the city. If I gaze far into the distance I can just see the silhouette of the area's most famous local landmark: the Angel of the North. I lift my binoculars for a closer look, and as I do so a distinctive, angular shape sweeps across my view in front of the sculpture: a red kite.

By rights, of course, red kites shouldn't be here in north-east England at all. Until a few years ago, the last time they had bred here was in the early nineteenth century. As Keith points out in what I imagine is a well-rehearsed speech, his great-grandfather wouldn't have seen kites here on Tyneside, his grandfather wouldn't have, and his dad certainly didn't. When he was a lad back in the 1970s the nearest kites were somewhere in mid-Wales, which as he puts it, 'might as well have been on the other side of the moon . . .'

The people of Newcastle and Gateshead are now getting used to seeing red kites on a daily basis. Kites soar in the skies over Europe's biggest shopping mall, the Metro Centre. Their high-pitched cries can be heard above the Tyne Bridge, Sage Concert Hall and Baltic Arts Centre. Best of all, the local bus company has repainted all its buses in the livery of this majestic raptor – not just a discreet red-kite symbol, but the whole bus, sides, back and front decked out as a giant bird of prey. The way local people have embraced the kites, and taken these new arrivals to their hearts, marks a huge change in attitudes towards birds of prey over the past few decades; a change that can only benefit Britain's wildlife as a whole.

❈

THERE ARE SOME parts of Britain that, to put it politely, you wouldn't expect to see in the tourist brochures. Canvey Island, on the edge of Essex, is one of them.

It's hard to imagine now, but in the early years of the twentieth century Canvey Island was Britain's fastest-growing seaside resort. Its proximity to London, one of the driest and sunniest climates in Britain, and a belief that the Essex air had healing properties all contributed to its brief heyday of popularity and prosperity. Amusement arcades, casinos, cafés and nightclubs were built, and the island attracted tens of thousands of day, weekend and holiday visitors.

But two unexpected factors brought an end to the Canvey Island gold rush. First, the terrible North Sea floods of early 1953, which devastated the east coast of England, and caused the deaths of almost 60 islanders and the temporary evacuation of 13,000 others. Then, from the late 1960s onwards, the rise of the foreign package holiday, which meant that instead of heading east, Londoners flew south to Spain. When it came to competing with the Costa del Sol and Costa Brava, Canvey Island was always going to be the loser.

Today, the island is a shadow of its former self. Peeling paint, boarded-up premises and a deserted seafront, together with a lingering reputation for crime, vandalism and extreme right-wing politics, all mean that Canvey frequently features on blogs and in articles as one of the worst places to live in Britain.

But the wildlife takes a rather different view. On a warm June day, adders and common lizards bask on jagged lumps of concrete, while marbled white butterflies show off their dappled wings as they flutter to feed on rose campion, an escaped garden plant now thriving in the wild, whose flowers glow shocking pink in the midday sun. Flocks of linnets and goldfinches flit from bush to bush, calling to stay in touch with one another as they go; while broad-bodied chasers – chunky, thickset dragonflies with bright yellow go-faster stripes along their sides – patrol the waterways like miniature First World War biplanes ready for a dogfight.

Turning a corner, I stumble across a real surprise: a damp, grassy area covered with marsh orchids, their flowers dappled white and pink. On one of the tallest blooms a plump, tawny-coloured bumblebee, with a banded abdomen like a cummerbund, is feeding greedily on nectar, probing deep into the flowers with its long tongue. To my untrained eye it looks like one of the commoner species, but a closer examination reveals that it is something much more interesting: a brown-banded carder bee.

This modest-looking insect is a real find here: one of the many casualties of intensive farming, it has vanished from most of Britain, and is now confined to the coastal fringes of southern and eastern England. But it has found a refuge in some unexpected places, including the land around the O2 Arena (formerly the Millennium Dome) in east London, as well as here on the Essex coast.

This is Canvey Wick, Britain's first official brownfield nature reserve. 'Brownfield' is defined as former industrial land awaiting development; and in the case of Canvey Wick, the site had been waiting to be developed for almost forty years, before it was finally saved for nature. Back in the early 1970s, an oil refinery was planned here, with the concrete foundations being dug and laid, and huge metal storage tanks installed. Then came the oil crisis of 1973, bringing a temporary halt on imports and widespread fuel rationing, and the project was summarily cancelled.

The land was set aside for redevelopment, but somehow this never happened. Meanwhile, nature began filling the vacuum left behind, and three decades later, the area was officially designated as a nature reserve, in recognition of its unique fauna and flora.

It may cover an area of just 100 hectares (less than half a square mile) yet it is home to more than 1,300 species of plants and animals. With more species of invertebrates than any other site apart from the east Kent promontory of Dungeness, it has earned the accolade of 'England's rainforest'. This may perhaps be a slight exaggeration, but it is not entirely unwarranted, considering the abundance of plant and animal life found here.

The reason why Canvey Wick is so good for wildlife is simple: unlike the wider countryside, which has been homogenised as a result of intensive farming, this site contains a broad mosaic of habitats in a very small space: including ditches, marshes, stony ground, meadows and grasslands, each of which offers niches for different plants and animals. And unlike farmland, it hasn't been covered with chemical fertilisers and pesticides, so that less competitive plants are able to survive and thrive.

What the story of Canvey Wick tells us is that when politicians and planners, and organisations such as the Campaign to Protect Rural England (CPRE) talk glibly about building on brownfield sites – as opposed to 'the countryside' – we may need to persuade them to think again. For many of Britain's plants and animals rely on places such as these: forgotten tracts of land, often dismissed as 'wasteland', which have been subject to a process best described as benign neglect. People enjoy them too – local wildlife groups now take parties of schoolchildren around Canvey Wick, opening their eyes to nature on their doorstep.

It's easy to forget that much of our lowland countryside is so intensively farmed that it supports very little in the way of specialised wildlife. So saving brownfield sites like this is crucial, if we are not to lose some of our most precious places and their unique mix of wild creatures.

❀

MANY OF THE stories in this chapter involve the accidental advantage taken by nature of an unusual situation; but few are quite so counter-intuitive as the notion that military sites – including training areas and firing ranges – could be any good for wildlife. The idea that an area where tanks roam over the land, crushing everything in their path, and where thousands of soldiers yomp over fields, with shells and bullets fired in a cacophony of noise, could ever be a place for nature, is hard to accept.

Yet right in the heart of southern Britain, one such place exists: a place that shows us just how diverse our wildlife could have been, had we not set out to ruin the countryside in our headlong quest for cheap food. That place is Salisbury Plain.

Stretching over 300 square miles, mainly in the county of Wiltshire (but extending into Hampshire), Salisbury

Plain is a vast, windswept chalk plateau – the largest area of chalk grassland in north-west Europe. It is best known for the ancient site of Stonehenge, lying on its south-eastern edge, just off the A303 trunk road to the West Country.

Many of the chalk downlands surrounding the plain have long since been turned over to intensive arable and dairy farming, losing their unique fauna and flora for ever. But thanks to the presence of Britain's largest military training area, much of Salisbury Plain has kept its original character; and so has also retained much of its wildlife.

The military arrived here just in time, at the very end of the nineteenth century. Had they come just a few decades later, the area would already have been ruined by intensive farming; but fortunately they took over before the post-war agricultural revolution, and so the unique fauna and flora survived.

At the height of summer, a visit to the heart of Salisbury Plain really is like taking a journey back in time. Hay meadows stretch in every direction, filled with displays of grasses and wild flowers to make your heart sing. These ancient grasslands are thronged with insects – beetles, bumblebees and gaudy day-flying moths, such as the slate-grey and crimson six-spot burnet. Little and barn owls are often seen by day as well as by night, taking advantage of the glut of small mammals, beetles and earthworms, perching on the gun turrets of tanks, and nesting in the hollows of oak trees dotted along the hedgerows.

From dawn to dusk, the song of skylarks fills the air, while whitethroats chatter noisily from the hedgerows, and yellowhammers sing their 'little-bit-of-bread-and-no-cheeese' song all around. Meanwhile a whinchat – one of the few still breeding in southern England – hops up onto a fence post, showing off his smart orange-and-buff breeding plumage and creamy eye stripe, before flitting away to feed.

As I walk through the long grass, I soon discover that the meadow is also thronged with butterflies. These include some of our scarcest and most threatened species: those that depend on unimproved chalk grassland, the dominant habitat here. A small blue – Britain's smallest and most delicate butterfly, with a wingspan of less than an inch across – perches on a flower, revealing its powder-blue underwings dotted with black. Small coppers, dapper in orange and chocolate brown, dazzling chalkhill blues, and a range of commoner species, all flutter across the meadow as far as the eye can see.

But the butterfly I am searching for is even scarcer than these. The marsh fritillary is a small insect – orange, cream and dark brown in colour – named after a Latin word meaning 'chequered'. Marsh fritillaries are fussy little things. They spend their whole lives in a little patch of grassland no bigger than a couple of football pitches. And like many of our scarcer butterflies, their young feed on just one specific plant, in this case, devil's-bit scabious.

Devil's-bit scabious is a tall, slender plant of the teasel family, with long stems and round, purple flowers. It grows on rough grasslands, often in damper areas, and prefers chalky soils. The unusual name is because when the roots are pulled up they are shorter than you might expect – leading to the widespread myth that they have been bitten off by the devil himself.

It is one of the first plants to colonise newly disturbed areas of ground, which is where the military comes in. The deep, rutted tracks left by passing tanks, and the shell craters remaining after explosions, are ideal for devil's-bit scabious; because the topsoil has been removed, there are fewer seeds from competing plants to get in first.

Also, because the whole area isn't sprayed with fertiliser, vigorous grasses struggle to survive in the poor soil. But for the devil's-bit scabious, the situation is ideal. By getting in early, it is able to grow to a decent size and support dozens, sometimes even hundreds, of marsh fritillary caterpillars.

That's what makes it so attractive to this little butterfly, which lays clumps of tiny, maroon-coloured eggs on the undersides of the long green leaves. When the eggs hatch into caterpillars, the devil's-bit scabious provides exactly what they need. The caterpillars immediately set to work, devouring the very plant they live on, and eating many times their own weight in leaves before pupating for the autumn and winter, and emerging as a butterfly the following spring.

❀

NEAR ST AUSTELL in Cornwall, 150 miles to the west of Salisbury Plain, several massive geometric domes rise up from the rolling landscape like alien spacecraft. They belong to the Eden Project.

This used to be an old china-clay quarry – a classic 'brownfield site'. But instead of simply filling it in and building a housing estate, as often happens, the developers here were rather more imaginative. This was mostly down to the vision of one man, the Eden Project's founder, Tim Smit, who realised that something wholly new and different could be created here.

Completed at the turn of the millennium, the state-of-the-art spheres, known as 'biomes', are made from huge, geometric plastic panels supported by sturdy steel frames. Housing thousands of different plant species from around the world, the spheres are each designed to recreate a specific natural environment – one representing the tropics, the other the Mediterranean. So it jars a little to hear recordings of birdsong, especially when you realise that the species you are listening to is not tropical at all, but a native British species: the robin.

Except that this isn't a recording at all, but the real thing. As I sit with my cappuccino and croissant in the café inside the dome, an actual, live robin hops down onto the table, cocking his head inquisitively towards me as if asking for some crumbs to eat. Everything about this bird is guaranteed to charm: his perky stance, poised with legs held slightly apart, flicking his tail and wings and flitting a foot or two towards me. The beady black eye, plump body and of course that orange breast (why the robin is named 'redbreast' is a bit of a mystery, given its actual colour) all come together to enchant and entrance me. He moves stealthily forward and snatches a morsel of pastry before rapidly flying away to devour his prize.

Robins aren't meant to be living inside the dome – the idea was to create an entirely self-contained world. But now that these birds have found their way in, the powers that be have tolerated their presence here; while the visitors seem delighted to come across a familiar friend in this rather alien environment.

What's really unusual about the robins living inside these domes is that they have changed their behaviour. Despite their endearing appearance, robins are well known to be feisty little birds, which habitually engage in territorial disputes with rival males, resulting in fights and sometimes even the death of one of the combatants. Yet here, the robins are friendly, sociable and apparently getting on with their neighbours. Maybe by being released from the pressures of finding food and avoiding predators, they are finally able to relax.

The robin isn't the only bird to have entered this artificial world. Blackbirds and blue tits, wrens and song thrushes, have all squeezed through the shell of the spheres and found their way inside, and the dome echoes with their songs and calls. Once here, there's no need to worry about bad weather, and no predators to threaten their eggs or chicks. For any bird able to get inside, this truly is Eden.

❀

THE WAY THESE birds – and all the other plants and animals in this chapter – have adapted to their new and totally artificial environments sums up the resourcefulness of Britain's wild creatures. For the past few centuries they have had to cope with constant changes that we've made to the landscape; changes that haven't always been for the best. Many have fallen by the wayside, but some, like the robins of the Eden Project, have managed to change their behaviour and take advantage of a wholly unexpected opportunity.

But although these 'accidental habitats' do matter, they are never going to be enough. However much they provide necessary refuges for nature, and even though they allow us to engage with wildlife in new and unexpected ways, they can only ever really be an 'added extra' to safeguarding our nation's natural heritage.

So we now face a simple choice; one that will dictate the future of Britain's wildlife. We can carry on as we have done since the end of the Second World War, using and abusing the land in pursuit of self-interest and short-term profit, with no real thought for the consequences for the wild creatures with which we share it. Or we can harness our ingenuity and imagination to create something new, ambitious, exciting, and on a truly grand scale.

The good news is that finally, at what really is the eleventh hour for Britain's countryside and its wildlife, we are at last beginning to fight back. Now, for the first time in the many thousands of years since our ancestors first settled on this little cluster of islands on the edge of Europe, we are deliberately creating new habitats where wildlife can thrive. And just as wildlife seems remarkably adept at finding a place to live – even when we least expect it – so when we actually create the ideal place for wild creatures to thrive, many will seize the opportunity to do so.

8

Back to the Future?

Wetlands and Rewilding

By what men think, we create the world around us, daily new.

Marion Zimmer Bradley, *The Mists of Avalon* (1982)

WATER TRULY IS the stuff of life. Apart from a few anaerobic bacteria, virtually all the terrestrial life forms on this planet – including, of course, human beings – depend for their survival on a constant supply of fresh, clean water. All wild creatures need water to drink and bathe, while many others – the wetland specialists – rely on it as a place to live.

Our lakes, ponds, bogs and marshes are lush, fertile habitats, bursting with a wealth of wildlife: from warblers to water voles, egrets to eels, and great crested newts to great crested grebes. Yet these wetlands are also incredibly fragile. They can be destroyed in an instant, by draining away the water to create new land for farming, homes, roads and industry. This, of course, is nothing new. Indeed, our wetlands have been under threat for longer than any other habitat. Very early on in the settlement of these islands, the more entrepreneurial of our ancestors came to regard wetlands as standing in the way of progress and development, and a lot more valuable if they could be transformed into drier agricultural land.

At first, they could do little to stop the seasonal flooding of their homes and fields; the power of the water was simply too much for their primitive technology. But as time went on, skills and expertise were developed to allow larger areas to be drained. They began to systematically reclaim these water-soaked lands, installing powerful pumps and digging a network of interconnected ditches and dykes to drain the water away, turning bog into barley field, marsh into meadow, and fen into farmland.

Before the draining began, places such as the Somerset Levels and the Great Fen – a huge wetland that covered much of low-lying East Anglia – were home to a vast array of wildlife. This included many creatures that eventually disappeared from Britain, such as cranes, avocets, beavers and bitterns. Others did survive, but in much lower numbers than in their heyday, including otters, wild swans, geese and ducks, the spectacle and numbers of which we can only begin to imagine.

In many ways the draining of these wetlands was the first – and arguably one of the worst – environmental disasters in Britain's history. But incredibly, despite all the pressures to develop lowland England for farming and building, a few small and scattered patches of this wetland habitat did manage to survive.

Today, as I make the long, steep climb up to the summit of Glastonbury Tor, I can gaze over mile after mile of this soggy landscape – the watery wonderland of the Somerset Moors and Levels. It's a place steeped in history, and also in controversy, for this is where some of the worst floods ever to hit Britain happened during the winter of 2012–13. But it is also a place of hope. For after centuries of neglect, our wetlands are now being reborn. Here in the heart of the West Country, in the land of cider, peat and willow, the tide may finally be turning, allowing our unique wetland wildlife to make a long-overdue comeback.

❀

ON A WARM Sunday afternoon towards the end of April, the long, narrow path that bisects this vast wetland – the old railway line that once ran from Highbridge to Glastonbury, until axed by the infamous Lord Beeching – is heaving with life. Families out for a leisurely afternoon walk rub shoulders with hikers and cyclists, along with little groups of birders, drawn to this remarkable place by some of Britain's rarest and most exciting birds.

On either side of the path, I hear the echoing song of eight different species of warbler. Chiffchaffs constantly call out their name, while Gilbert White's other favourite, the willow warbler, sings his silvery descant in response. Blackcaps and garden warblers duet in the sallows, while whitethroats launch themselves into the air from the tops of brambles, their scratchy song matching their choice of home. In the reed beds themselves, the chuntering of reed warblers is countered by the more excitable performance of their cousin the sedge warbler; while in the dense, scrubby vegetation alongside, shouted snatches of song from the impossibly loud Cetti's warbler are the only clue to this skulking bird's presence.

In the rapidly warming air above, male and female marsh harriers are indulging in their courtship display: the smaller male flying over his mate and then dropping her a parcel of food – a vole, perhaps, or a small bird – which she catches with acrobatic grace. Higher still, hobbies – sleek and streamlined falcons just returned from Africa – snatch airborne insects with a practised sweep from claws to beak. Amongst them, the even more streamlined swifts, the first to return this spring, are swooping and screaming as if full of joy to be back.

Then a much larger bird takes to the wing from deep inside the reed bed: tall, slender, and white as a ghost. An excited shout goes up from a watching birder, causing momentary panic amongst the passers-by. Only then does he realise that calling out 'great white!' might not be the wisest choice of words, and that perhaps he should have added the word 'egret' to his announcement.

The great white egret flaps slowly but strongly up into the air, neck arched like a snake, long legs stretched out behind. A metre high, this is our tallest heron; not far short of the crane, its rival for the title of Britain's tallest bird. This one's jet-black bill and wispy plumes show that it is in full breeding plumage (the bill turns custard yellow in autumn and winter), while two coloured plastic rings on its legs reveal its identity.

This is a female, which arrived here as an adult in 2010, having been ringed as a nestling the year before in the Loire-Atlantique *département* of western France. Having flown more than 600 miles to the north-west, this pioneering waterbird ended up here on the Somerset Levels. She liked what she saw, stayed, and in 2012 she, her mate and another pair nested here and raised five young between them. This was not just the first breeding record for Somerset, but the first in recorded history anywhere in Britain.

Great white egrets aren't the only new arrivals. Bearded tits – glorious little birds with Fu Manchu moustaches and a delicate plumage of greyish-mauve and orange – ping like old-fashioned cash registers in the reeds; while occasionally a flock of cranes, long-necked, wide-winged and honking like tuneful geese, pass high overhead on their springtime wanderings.

None of these birds would have been here even a decade ago, while other creatures such as otters and water voles have made a comeback as well. Harvest mice build their tiny grass nests in the damp meadows, and butterflies thrive in the wet woods of alder, birch and willow: the oak-loving purple hairstreak, the magnificent white admiral, and the delicate orange-and-black silver-washed fritillary, which floats serenely along wooded rides on warm June days.

But most importantly of all, the return of the wildlife has also attracted people. From the surrounding towns and villages, and from much further afield, they now come to witness a miracle in the making: the rewilding of the Avalon Marshes. These people will ultimately be the key to the success or failure of the most exciting project to restore a landscape for wildlife currently taking place anywhere in Britain.

❀

NOT SO LONG ago – just over a decade at most, only one member of the heron family bred in Somerset: the familiar grey heron. For much of the twentieth century only two species – the grey heron and the bittern – bred in the whole of Britain. Today five herons – grey heron, bittern, little bittern, little egret and great white egret – breed here regularly, and a sixth (cattle egret) has bred in the recent past, and may well do so again in the near future. Another long-legged waterbird, the crane, has been successfully reintroduced to the southern part of the Levels, while several others, including purple heron, night heron, glossy ibis and white stork, are rare but regular visitors here.

I first encountered a little egret in Britain in the summer of 1970, when I was an eager young birder visiting Brownsea Island in Dorset. I can still remember the sense of surprise and excitement when I opened up the shutters of a hide and saw this Persil-white apparition perched on a branch across the lake. I didn't see another little egret in this country until the late 1980s, the point at which these elegant birds – once only sighted on trips to the Mediterranean – began their permanent colonisation of Britain.

Since then, they have become a common and familiar bird, with almost 1000 breeding pairs: a remarkable expansion given that the very first pair nested (coincidentally on Brownsea Island) as recently as 1996. To put this into perspective, there are considerably more little egrets breeding in Britain than there are choughs, wigeons, marsh harriers or bearded tits. Great white egrets used to be an even rarer bird here: back in the 1970s they nested no nearer to Britain than Lake Neusiedl in Austria. But like the little egret they too have expanded their range northwards and westwards, colonising France and the Netherlands before they arrived in southern England.

So why have these new colonists arrived; and how have they managed to gain a foothold so rapidly? Climate change is undoubtedly a factor: many of these species have been rapidly expanding their ranges northwards through Europe in the past couple of decades. Another reason waterbirds are able to expand their range so rapidly is that they are sociable birds, which breed – and usually migrate – in groups. Birds of other species that travel singly may reach Britain, but may then be unable to find a mate; whereas herons and egrets usually arrive in flocks, so can pair up and breed immediately.

Yet we cannot simply ascribe the success of these waterbirds to factors such as climate change or natural range expansion. The final piece of the jigsaw is the habitat itself: had they arrived here half a century ago they would never have colonised, for there wouldn't have been anywhere to build a nest and find enough food to raise a family.

And however 'natural' the Avalon Marshes appear, this is quite definitely an artificial, post-industrial and almost entirely man-made landscape, constructed from what was left behind after thousands of tonnes of peat had been removed. This is where a small group of ambitious, far-sighted conservationists enter the story. On the BBC1 series 'Britain's Big Wildlife Revival', the RSPB's Tony Whitehead recalls when the organisation first acquired land at what was to become the Avalon Marshes:

> I remember in the mid-1990s it was just fields and these huge peat-black holes in the ground. There had been much debate about what to do with these – boating lakes perhaps, or landfill sites

for the nearby city of Bristol? Fortunately for us, they were chosen to become nature reserves. But they looked nothing like nature reserves to start off with!

The RSPB, along with other conservation organisations such as the Somerset Wildlife Trust, realised that this landscape of redundant peat diggings was not a blight, but an opportunity. For when the peat has been removed, there's very little you can do with the holes in the ground that remain. You can't fill them in again – it would be impossibly impractical and expensive to transport so many thousands of tonnes of soil – so you can't build homes on them or turn them back into farmland.

What you can do is create a new wetland habitat: put in reeds to make reed beds, and then sit back and let nature do the rest. And that's exactly what they did. An army of volunteers, guided by professional scientists and conservationists, planted thousands of reeds in their greenhouses and then put them into the watery ground by hand. Very soon – much quicker, indeed, than anyone expected – the landscape began to soften at the edges and appear more natural. Insects, plants, amphibians, birds and mammals returned, finding a haven where they could seek out safe places to breed, feed and hide from predators.

But perhaps the greatest success story is that of a bird we rarely see: a bird proverbially shy and elusive, whose presence is often only given away by its incredible booming call. This deep, resonant sound can carry as far as 5 miles, further than any bird in the world. It's made by the bittern.

❀

IT TOOK ME almost twenty years to see a bittern, and it certainly wasn't for want of trying. As a teenage birder, year after year I would hitchhike, cycle or cadge a lift to some of the best places to find bitterns in Britain: the RSPB reserves at Minsmere in Suffolk and Titchwell in Norfolk; the marshlands around the River Stour at Stodmarsh in East Kent; and the legendary reserve at Cley on the North Norfolk coast. Yet try as I might, I never saw a single one.

When a bittern poses in its reed-bed habitat you can sometimes stare right at it and yet still not see the bird at all. They are the shade and colour of mature reeds: vertical streaks of black, brown and buff providing perfect camouflage. They rarely move, and hardly ever fly; even if they do it is usually only for a few seconds, so that by the time someone has spotted a bittern, realised what it is and called out its name, the bird has dropped back down into the reeds. The usual impression is of a short-necked, rather ungainly bird, memorably described by one young observer as looking like 'a toasted heron'.

By the time I was in my early twenties I had given up any hope of ever catching up with this mysterious creature; indeed, I was beginning to doubt its very existence. Then, on a casual walk around Leighton Moss on the edge of Morecambe Bay in Lancashire, I noticed what looked like an old coat draped over a post by the edge of a reed bed, about a quarter of a mile away. I casually lifted my binoculars and the coat/post moved, stepping gingerly forward, before melting back into the reed bed, to be seen no more.

For a moment, I thought I was hallucinating, and had imagined the whole bizarre scene. But this was indeed my very first bittern. My duck, as it were, had been broken, and over the next twenty years or so I saw a few more, though never very well: usually as they posed momentarily by a dense stand of reeds, or flew a few feet over the reed bed before plunging back down again.

During the summer of 2006, I moved to Somerset. That very year a pair of bitterns bred on the Avalon Marshes for the first time since the 1960s. The following year, a few more pairs arrived, and now, nearly a decade later, there are almost fifty booming males in this newly created wetland. And unlike the secretive bitterns of East Anglia, these are true extroverts.

When my son George was five years old, we went for a walk along the old railway line that spans the nature reserves. During the next couple of hours we saw no fewer than seven bitterns: some posed on the reeds, others flying straight overhead, giving us amazing views. When the seventh, and last, bird passed a few yards over our heads, I excitedly grabbed George's arm and pointed it out. He shrugged casually, as if to say, 'Bittern? But they're really common . . .'

And to be fair, he had a point. One June day when I was on the Avalon Marshes from early morning until late evening, I had at least sixteen sightings of bitterns, including four (presumably two pairs) grappling with one another overhead. The volunteers at the RSPB watchpoint have done even better – one Saturday they totted up more than forty sightings by teatime.

The high visibility of these normally shy birds is likely to be down to several different factors. The main one is that bitterns are so common here – the numbers packed in so densely – that the odds are firmly in favour of seeing at least one or two on a typical visit. That's especially true in May and June when the adults are flying off to find food for their young, hidden safe inside the middle of the reed bed.

But there may be another factor at work. The very first bitterns turned up here in winter, suggesting that perhaps they didn't come from East Anglia, where the population is fairly sedentary, but from further afield, for instance Germany or the Netherlands. Perhaps these Continental birds are less shy than their reserved English cousins. Whatever the reason, increasing numbers of people are enjoying more and better views of these amazing birds than ever before – and the species is doing so well that there are now as many bitterns in this little corner of Somerset as in the whole of East Anglia.

❀

BITTERNS AND OTHER waterbirds are doing pretty well on that side of the country too, thanks to another ambitious wetland restoration scheme. The Great Fen Project began in the late 1990s, when plans were first made to link two of the oldest nature reserves in Britain, Holme and Woodwalton Fens.

This isn't the only successful wetland-restoration project in East Anglia. Nearby, on the borders of Norfolk and Suffolk, between the villages of Lakenheath and Hockwold cum Wilton, the RSPB has converted 300 hectares of intensively farmed arable land into a wetland wonderland: Lakenheath Fen. Less than two decades after work began, the site is now a mixture of reed beds, grazing marshes and open pools, a recreation of the fenland that would once have been here.

The results have been truly breathtaking. Where once a handful of reed warblers sang their rhythmic song, there are now more than 400 pairs; where carrots were once planted and harvested, marsh harriers cruise, bitterns boom and bearded tits deliver their ringing, metallic call. And in 2009 a pair of common cranes successfully nested here, rearing two young, which apart from a failed attempt two years earlier was the first time this mighty species had bred in the East Anglian Fens for over 400 years.

The former chief executive of the RSPB, Baroness Barbara Young of Old Scone, was once asked the secret of the success of these wetland-restoration projects. Her reply – 'Just add water' – may have appeared flippant, but it does sum up the extraordinary speed with which deeply unpromising locations such as old peat diggings and carrot fields can be transformed into productive places for nature.

❀

THE STARK TRUTH is that while wetlands are relatively easy to recreate in a matter of just a few years, getting the countryside right for a myriad of other species – especially those that depend on traditional farmland, managed woodland or the uplands – is far more difficult. But we must do so. As the environment continues to change with a rapidity never seen before – especially as the less benevolent effects of global climate change take hold – we cannot afford to rely on old-style conservation measures, such as nature reserves, to safeguard our natural heritage.

Nature reserves have a long and distinguished history. At the start of the twentieth century, when the main threat to birds and other wildlife was persecution, it made perfect sense to fence off small parcels of good-quality land, to safeguard the species living there.

Over time, this developed into the policy of protecting and helping 'flagship species' –rare and showy birds such as the osprey and avocet – which could then be held up as examples of why a particular habitat needed to be preserved. This was based on a very pragmatic principle: that it is much easier to get public support for saving the avocet than the angle shades moth, or the capercaillie than *Callicera rufa*, a scarce species of hoverfly found only in the Caledonian pine forest – an insect so obscure it doesn't even have an English name. But the trouble with this approach was that while it worked well in terms of PR, encouraging visitors and gaining new members for the various conservation charities, it failed in three crucial respects.

First, it meant that when unexpected environmental changes began to occur as a result of climate change – such as a rise in sea levels or an increase in the incidence and severity of coastal storms – many of the best-known reserves turned out to be very vulnerable because of their prime position on the east coast of England. Thus Minsmere, Titchwell and Cley – flagship reserves that between them attract hundreds of thousands of visitors each year – have all recently suffered from flooding and habitat destruction following severe autumn and winter storms.

Second, it meant that although we can point to a whole raft of success stories for rare creatures – those that thrived in the specialised habitats found on nature reserves – we have inadvertently allowed some of our commonest species to enter a spiral of decline; a decline from which some may not be able to recover. Birds such as the skylark, starling and house sparrow, mammals like the hedgehog and water vole, and many common butterflies including the small tortoiseshell have all experienced big falls in numbers in recent years – and of course these species don't only live on nature reserves, but also out in the wider countryside.

By protecting tiny, albeit biologically significant, areas of Britain, while allowing vast swathes of the rural environment to be destroyed, damaged or degraded, we have stood by while these familiar wild creatures, some so familiar that perhaps we took them for granted, have plummeted in numbers. Despite the many success stories – which we can and should celebrate – and the crucial importance of nature reserves as a potential reservoir for restocking the wider countryside, our fauna and flora are more impoverished now than at any time in our human history on these islands.

But it is the third, unintended consequence of the pre-eminence of nature reserves that strikes me as the most important. The attitude of their owners and managers to the general public – even in relatively recent times – has contributed to the marginalisation of the natural world and its low importance on the political and economic agenda. For when these nature reserves were set up, the last thing their wardens wanted was people trampling all over their precious habitat and disturbing their rare and vulnerable wildlife.

When I wanted to visit the RSPB's reserve at Minsmere in 1973, my mother had to write several months in advance to request a permit; and even then numbers were limited and the reserve itself was only open for a few days of the week. Things have of course improved a lot since then; by and large nature reserves now welcome visitors, and have done an awful lot to encourage newcomers, especially families, to visit. My old friend the late Derek Moore, to whom this book is dedicated, started this off back in the 1980s when, as the newly installed chief executive of the Suffolk Wildlife Trust, he proposed open access to all the organisation's nature reserves. Despite opposition from those who thought this would be a disaster, as people would no longer bother to join the trust if they could gain access for free, the scheme proved to be a huge success; attracting new members and placing nature firmly in the public eye. Today, virtually all nature reserves in Britain allow free entry.

Nevertheless, there is still a residual reluctance to visit amongst the vast majority of the population, for whom a day out on a nature reserve is only marginally more likely than a trip to the moon. Whether they think they won't be wearing the right clothes or carrying the right equipment; whether they cannot get to what are, after all, mainly hard-to-reach rural locations; or whether, as I suspect, they simply think that nature isn't for them, they are not choosing to spend time in these places.

Nor are they joining the organisations that run them. Although the total membership of the National Trust, RSPB and Wildlife Trusts now tops 6 million (not accounting for those who are members of more than one organisation), that still leaves close to 60 million people who are not members – about 90 per cent of the British population as a whole.

❁

So what can we do to change both attitudes and practices when it comes to safeguarding our natural heritage? Schemes such as the Great Fen Project and Somerset's Avalon Marshes – those that engage local people to transform places for wildlife, and do so on a vast and ambitious scale – are crucial if we are to stem the tide of decline. But we need to go even further: to reintegrate nature into people's lives by making room for wildlife right across both urban and rural Britain. From the banks of our city rivers to farmers' fields, and from the highest mountaintops to the tidelines around our coasts, we need to allow nature to come back.

Fortunately, conservationists are now, at last, beginning to realise the error of their ways and think big – really big. Today the primary focus is on what are called 'landscape-scale' projects: joining up existing sites for wildlife and creating new ones from scratch, in order to provide the kind of habitat that will function on the scale needed to bring back our wildlife. It's time, say the conservationists, to stop arguing about the small details and create places where people and wildlife can coexist to the benefit of all.

This process is often known as 'rewilding' – an evocative yet somewhat misleading term, as it suggests returning to some distant, Eden-like state where birds and beasts roamed the land untouched and unaffected by human influence. Romantics have embraced this concept with open arms, some seeing it as an opportunity to take human beings out of the equation altogether. Humans, they argue, have messed things up enough; now what we need is to let vast swathes of the landscape go back to nature, allowing natural processes of growth and succession to triumph, without the dread hand of human intervention.

It is a seductive argument. After all, it can easily be claimed that because we have done so much damage in the past, it is now time to leave Mother Nature alone, and let her regenerate our landscape and renew its damaged wildlife. It could even work: providing, that is, nature didn't have to share our small island with close to 70 million people; and if we didn't mind waiting a few hundred, or in some cases a few thousand, years.

Fortunately, however, there is a third way. Rather than simply leaving things as they are and wringing our hands as our natural heritage continues to decline, or shutting humans out to allow nature to take its revenge, like some sci-fi tale of the end of humanity, we can intervene intelligently on a large scale to recreate habitats and bring back lost wildlife.

This approach is already well under way just across the North Sea, in the Netherlands. We may think we live on a crowded island, but even with a population density half as great again as the UK, the Dutch have still managed to create a new area larger than all of Britain's wetlands put together. Begun in the late 1960s, Oostvaardersplassen now extends across an area of 5600 hectares (22 square miles), right in the middle of one of the most built-up areas of Europe. And this isn't just a place for wildlife – extensive networks of paths and tracks have ensured that millions of people are able to visit and enjoy this new wilderness in the very heart of the country.

We are already following suit – albeit on a smaller scale – with those wetland-restoration projects in East Anglia and on the Somerset Levels. We only need to take a global view to see that our wetlands need all the help they can get: for right across the world they are amongst the world's most threatened habitats. And as the world's climate continues to get warmer, and more and more people compete for even more limited water resources, this trend is likely to get worse long before it gets better.

New wetlands have many other benefits, too. They enable us to manage the effects of droughts, storms and floods; all likely outcomes of the more extreme weather events brought about by climate change; a particularly pertinent aspect of the Avalon Marshes restoration project in the heart of the Somerset Levels. And perhaps most importantly of all, they are great places to visit – providing better and deeper opportunities to engage people with wildlife in a more meaningful way. So creating these new habitats is important not just for birds, but for human beings too.

❀

COULD THIS APPROACH work in other habitats – especially in the two most damaged ones, farmland and woodland? It would certainly be harder to restore ancient woodlands than wetlands, not least because the timescale is so vastly different – as someone once remarked, when you rewild a woodland the first 500 years are the hardest. But slow and steady woodland-restoration projects have already borne fruit, even though they will take many decades to reach their peak.

At a dark time for farmland wildlife, one of the few small rays of light comes from a corner of Sussex, where a quiet revolution is under way on the Knepp Castle Estate. It's being masterminded by Sir Charles Burrell, 10th Baronet, who has turned 3,500 acres of formerly intensive farmland into one of the biggest and most ambitious rewilding experiments in Europe.

The Burrells have owned and worked this land for more than two centuries, but although he only succeeded to the baronetcy with the death of his father in 2008, Charlie Burrell has been managing the estate for more than thirty years. For the first decade or so, he continued to farm the land in the same way as his neighbours in Sussex and elsewhere in lowland Britain: intensively, with arable crops and dairy cattle. And yet he was still struggling to make a profit.

Then, a year after the turn of the millennium, in 2001, he had an epiphany, realising that if the land was ever to realise its full potential – for both farming and wildlife – he needed to step off the treadmill of highly intensive agriculture and try a very different approach: an approach that melded the traditional with the modern, and the complex with the very, very simple.

After removing 300 miles of fences to create one large estate rather than a series of small fields and enclosures, he brought in a range of large herbivores – including cows, horses and deer. The aim was to drive changes right across the estate, creating a mosaic of habitats where wildlife could thrive in all its amazing complexity, and also to provide high-quality meat to sell. These animals' grazing helps to create open grassland, areas of scrub, bare ground and forested groves, all carefully designed to maintain the balance between grassland and woodland and avoid either becoming dominant.

After little more than a decade, the results are stunning: the wildlife has returned in droves, with nightingales singing from every thicket, purple emperor butterflies dancing at the tops of the ancient oak trees, and a host of farmland flowers, insects, mammals and birds; just as there would have been in rural Sussex a century or more ago.

Rivers, urban areas and the 'accidental' habitats described in the last chapter require a different approach, in which linking up existing sites to create wildlife corridors is arguably more important than creating completely new habitats. But this too can be done remarkably quickly, as the restoration of our river wildlife has proved in the past few decades.

Our coastal habitats face a very different problem: the rise in sea levels and erosion caused by more frequent and severe storms make this perhaps our most urgent challenge. 'Managed retreat' is the new watchword, working with the sea rather than trying to hold it back. This approach is not without its drawbacks, as opponents point out, especially those who will have to sacrifice their land and homes to the new policy. But ultimately, by softening the boundaries between land and sea, and letting the water cover some land so that it does not cause greater damage and destruction elsewhere, our coastal communities and their wildlife will undoubtedly benefit.

There are precedents, not least the RSPB's reserve at Minsmere on the Suffolk coast, which was accidentally created when the land was flooded during the Second World War to prevent a German invasion. The most recent 'managed realignment' projects, all of which have already brought major benefits in terms of flood prevention, restoration of wildlife and habitat, and eco-tourism, include Medmerry on the Sussex coast, where the RSPB have worked with the Environment Agency to build a sea wall 2 kilometres inland to allow a low-lying area of land to flood as and when the sea surges occur; the Wallasea Island Wild Coast project in Essex, which will create 600 hectares (1,500 acres) of new wildlife habitat; and Steart Marshes in Somerset, where the Wildfowl and Wetlands Trust have worked closely with local residents to provide long-term protection to homes and farmland while also improving the area for migrant and wintering birds.

All these approaches – although they necessarily differ in detail – have two things in common. First, they take a pragmatic rather than a philosophical approach. As one conservationist told me, we have spent enough time debating the moral issues of whether rewilding constitutes 'meddling with nature', as some detractors have falsely claimed. Now we need to roll up our sleeves and do the hard work to restore the biodiversity that we ourselves have been responsible for diminishing.

The second thing they have in common is that they produce a tangible wildlife dividend – and often much more quickly than we might have assumed. Nature has proved remarkably resilient; once we have restored their habitats, wild creatures have rapidly seized the new opportunities.

❀

VERY FEW POLITICIANS or organisations are explicitly 'anti-nature'; most agree that it is by and large 'a good thing', so long as it doesn't get in the way of what they call progress. But when it comes to a bluebell wood versus a new bypass, the choice between singing nightingales and a housing estate, or bumblebees and butterflies against the need to squeeze even higher yields of crops from every last corner of the countryside, there can only be one winner – and it's not nature.

Although we as naturalists and conservationists would prefer to lay the blame elsewhere – on the farmers and developers, politicians and bureaucrats – we must all share some responsibility for what has happened on our watch. It was we as consumers who demanded cheaper and cheaper food, forcing farmers to choose industrial-scale agriculture over traditional, wildlife-friendly practices. It was we who turned a blind eye to the piecemeal destruction of many of those fragments of habitat that remained. And it was we who stood by while politicians paid lip service to 'the environment', while ignoring the problems of habitat loss, pollution and global climate change.

It wasn't so much that we took our eye off the ball; rather that our opponents were playing an entirely different game, using a completely new set of rules. Most of all, we got conservation policy wrong. In a last-ditch effort to save what we had left, we focused not on the commonplace, but on the rare. We fenced off little parcels of land and called them 'nature reserves', as if wildlife could be corralled into a separate space where it would somehow be shielded from what was happening elsewhere in our land.

So while we were making sure that avocets and ospreys were safe, the rest of our countryside was being trashed in the name of short-term profit. During this period, those who consider themselves the 'custodians of the countryside' – landowners, farmers' unions and self-appointed pressure groups among them – have wilfully turned a blind eye to the destruction, furthering their own shortsighted self-interest. This was not just at the expense of our wildlife, but also short-changed the millions of people in towns and cities who love and value the countryside, but have been told they can have no say in the way it is managed.

How do we solve this problem, and put wildlife back where it belongs – at the centre of our lives? One way is to give the natural world an economic value: to measure in monetary terms its contribution to the economy, as in the title of a timely book by environmentalist and author Tony Juniper, *What Has Nature Ever Done for Us?* This directly confronts those who regard nature conservation as somehow being a drag on the nation's economic growth, and points out the hidden value of 'ecosystem services': ways that natural habitats contribute to the economy and our wider well-being. Managing land for wildlife can prevent flooding, for example, as it has done here on the Somerset Levels; or bring much-needed revenue through wildlife tourism, as on the Isle of Mull, where people coming to see the nesting eagles contribute millions of pounds to the local economy.

Putting a value on wildlife and the places where it lives is a crucial piece of the jigsaw as we try to repair the damage that has been done; but it is still not enough. The other part of the solution is the process of landscape-scale conservation. That's what's going on down the road from me on the Avalon Marshes – and it's working. Now we need to think big: to roll out projects such as this – and the others I feature in this book – all over Britain. We have argued amongst ourselves for too long as to what works and what doesn't; now is the time for action to restore habitats and make room for wildlife on a nationwide scale, before it is too late.

To paraphrase the Hollywood movie *Field of Dreams*, 'Build it – and they will come.' And they have: every year now, growing numbers of people visit here to enjoy some of Britain's most spectacular wild creatures. In doing so, they pump money into the rural economy, improve their health and well-being, and above all enjoy a wonderful, life-enhancing experience. We can choose to destroy all this – as we have destroyed so much of Britain's landscape and wildlife – for short-term gain. Or we can embrace what has already been achieved, build on it, and watch with wonder as more and more wild creatures choose to return.

The Pelican's Return

By them sat the loving pelican,
Whose young ones, poison'd by the serpent's sting,
With her own blood again to life doth bring.

Michael Drayton

IF WE DELVE back into the distant past, we find one species of bird that could become the emblem of this rebirth of a landscape. It's a creature so rare, so magical, and so bizarre, that bringing it back here might be considered absurd. Yet it is also perfectly feasible to believe that – given time, effort and the will to recreate a wetland on a truly huge scale – it could return.

Several thousand years ago an Iron Age hunter – using a slingshot, perhaps – managed to kill a huge bird, a bird larger even than the great white egrets, bitterns and cranes that now fly over the Avalon Marshes. Two-and-a-half millennia later an archaeologist excavating a site on Glastonbury Tor unearthed the bones of that bird, and identified it as a Dalmatian pelican.

With a wingspan of more than 3.5 metres, and weighing as much as 15 kilos, the Dalmatian pelican is one of the heaviest flying birds in the world. It is also one of the most endangered. Once millions of these charismatic waterbirds thronged the wetlands of south-east Europe and western Asia, but fewer than 20,000 remain. It is now confined to a small swathe of land from eastern Europe, through Greece to western Russia; and like all wetland species it is extremely vulnerable to habitat loss and hunting.

But what if we could bring the Dalmatian pelican back to its ancestral home? Imagine a wetland large enough to support a bird with such a voracious appetite, with flocks of pelicans flying over Wells Cathedral, drifting over festival-goers at Glastonbury, or soaring high over the famous Tor. Imagine watching a raft of pelicans fishing in unison, dipping their beaks into the shallow waters like a team of synchronised swimmers, or the sound of those mighty wings as they fly in formation high overhead, their brilliant white plumage glistening in the summer sunshine.

Imagine a place that would also be the home to cranes and beavers, bitterns and egrets, otters and water voles, dragonflies and damselflies – and countless other wild creatures that depend on our magical wetlands. A place where people could encounter and experience wildlife in a way that truly enhances the quality of their lives. With imagination and vision we could create the biggest wetland in Western Europe – our very own version of the Florida Everglades, simply packed with wildlife. Now that really would be worth seeing.

Acknowledgements

MANY PEOPLE HAVE helped me with the writing of this book, generously offering their advice and expertise during the course of its genesis, writing and completion. I should like to thank John Aplin, Mark Avery, David Goode, Martin Harper, Rob Lambert, John Lister-Kaye, Rob Penn, Mark Robins, Kevin Rylands, Brett Westwood and Tony Whitehead. Any errors of fact are, it goes without saying, my own.

I should also like to thank the many people who gave up their time to show me around many of the special places featured in the book. They include Chris Knights, Nicholas Watts, David White, Matt Prior, Ken Greenway and Keith Bowey. Thanks too to my colleagues on *Britain's Big Wildlife Revival*, made by Outline Productions for BBC1, and my former colleagues at the BBC Natural History Unit.

A huge debt of thanks goes to three people. First and foremost, Rosemary Davidson of Square Peg, who commissioned the book and had the confidence to allow me to develop from the gentler side of nature writing to encompass a more opinionated and polemical approach. My dear friend Graham Coster offered his clear and perceptive opinions on the draft chapters, enabling me to cut to the chase more quickly, and produce a clearer and more structured narrative. My agent, Broo Doherty, encouraged me from the very beginning of the project and has been her usual wonderfully supportive self throughout.

At Square Peg and Vintage thank you to Mary Chamberlain for her incisive and brilliant copy-editing, to my proofreader Alex Milner, to Rowena Skelton-Wallace and to Simon Rhodes and Rachael Ludbrook in production and design.

I would also like to thank, as always, my dear wife Suzanne and my children David, James, Charlie, George and Daisy for their continued love and support.

Finally, this book is dedicated to my old friend and mentor Derek Moore. Before his untimely death, Derek spent his every waking hour fighting to save, support and encourage Britain's wildlife for others to enjoy. He was a shining light in a world where conformity often takes precedence over saying what we really think. Derek was never afraid to offend the vested interests standing in the way of wildlife conservation; yet he also worked closely with former adversaries to achieve real change.

I hope that some of Derek's fighting spirit influenced me while I was writing this book. He died far too young and I, and many others, miss him.